Never Too Young

How young children can take responsibility and make decisions

Judy Miller

We're the world's independent children's charity. We're outraged that millions of children are still denied proper healthcare, food, education and protection. We're working flat out to get every child their rights and we're determined to make further, faster changes. How many? How fast? It's up to you.

Published by
Save the Children
1 St John's Lane
London EC1M 4AR
UK
+44 (0)20 7012 6400
savethechildren.org.uk

First published by the National Early Years Network in association with Save the Children in 1997
This edition published by Save the Children 2003
Reprinted 2009

ISBN 1 84187 075 7

Cover photo: Teri Pengilley

Printed by Page Bros.

Contents

Introduction 5
Benefits of involving young children 5
Children's rights 6
What do we mean by participation? 6
Levels of participation 7
Participation in practice 8

How to use this handbook 9

**Section 1
Where do we start from? 11**

Attitudes to children 11
Generalisations 11
Turning into stereotypes 12

What is childhood? 12
Another view of childhood 12

The beginning of childhood 13
Home life 13
Play time 13
Working life 13
School life 14

A better childhood? 14
Why is it an insult to be childish? 14
The abuse of power over children 15
'Children should be seen and not heard' 15
'Adults know best' 15

Why it is important for children to participate 16
Benefits for children 16
Benefits for parents 16
Benefits for the group 16
Benefits for society 17

Barriers to participation 17
Attitudes 17
Expectations of children 17
Children who do not want to take part 17
Information 18
How things work 18
Access 19
Resources 19
Managing participation in a group 20

New ways of doing things 20
Power sharing 20
Communicating with parents 21

What does participation look like in practice? 21
What might happen – assessing the risks 21
At home 22
At playgroup 22
Judging children's capacity to participate 22
Desirable outcomes for children's learning 22

Preparing for participation 23
At what age can we expect children to ...? 24
0–18 months 24
1½–3½ years 25
3½–5 years 26
6–7 years 26

A policy for participation 27
Drawing up a policy 27
A suggested approach 27
Setting achievable goals 27
Implementing your policy 28
Making a plan of action 28
Monitoring your policy 28
Evaluating your policy 28

Action points checklist 29

**Section 2
How are children participating now? 30**

Talking and listening 31

Exploring children's perception of the rules 32

Conflict 32
Approaches to conflict 33
Mediation 33
Conflict between children and adults 33

Sharing 33
'You can't play' 34
'You can't say you can't play' 34

Caring and co-operation 35

Environment 35

Access 35
   A child's eye view 35
Making changes to the environment 36
Finding things 36
   Labelling 36
   Room arrangement 37

Daily routines and choice of activities 37

Routines that enable children to make choices 38
   A 'milk bar' system for snack times 38
   Alternative ways of resting 38
Making choices 38
   Free choice: *Schemas* 38
   Making choices within a system: *High/Scope* 39

Choosing equipment 41

Monitoring use of the equipment 42
   Consulting children on upgrading playgrounds 42

Food 43

Encouraging a positive attitude to food 43
Planning menus 44
   Finding out what foods children like 44
   Choosing from these options 44

**Section 3
Participation – how to do it 46**

Getting started 46

Finding out what is important for children 46

Participatory techniques 49

Activities to develop confidence and self-esteem 50
   Photo displays 50
   Self-portraits 50
   Badges 50
Activities and games to develop group co-operation 51
   Group mimes 51
   Individual mimes 51
   Problem mimes 51
   Pass the mask 51
   Touch a shoe 52
   Centre throw 52
   Circular chair 52
   Farmyard animals 52
Activities to facilitate discussion 53
   Circle Time 53
   Brainstorming 54

Expressing feelings and opinions 55
   All About Me books 55
   Telling and acting out children's own stories 56
   Feelings – drama 57
   When you ... I felt 57
   Feelings – photographs 57
   Musical feelings – exploring how children feel about given situations 58
   Happy lines/sad lines 58
   Happy mats/sad mats 59
   Happy trains/sad trains 59
   Thumbs up/thumbs down 59
   Happy masks/sad masks 59
Making choices 60
   Pros and cons 60
   Toy catalogue 61
   Toy shop 61
Exploring specific issues 63
   Looking at conflict – using puppets 63
   Looking at conflict – using stories 63
   Looking at rules – the 'naughty puppet' 63
   Looking at rules – the fishing game 64
   Looking at rules – a card game 64
   Who we like to be with – 1 65
   Who we like to be with – 2 65
   Adult roles 66
   Designing a play area 67
Evaluating the group 68
   Questionnaire 68
   Taped interviews 68
   Good things/bad things 69
   Picture game – to find out what children think about the activities 69
   Beans in jars – quantitative evaluation 70
   Me at nursery (playgroup/childminder) 70

Appendix: Legislation concerning children's employment and education – a summary 71

References 72

Introduction

'It's not fair!' protested William. 'The big people are doing what they like, but they won't let us do what we like. They think that because we're small we don't have brains. But we do – we've got big brains! What I think is people's brains get smaller when they grow up.'

A six year old reached this conclusion. In spite of lengthy negotiations, the grown-ups had insisted he was 'too small' to join other children playing on bales of hay in the field next to the pub where their parents were drinking.

William, it has to be said, was overstating his case. His parents treat him with respect, listen to his views and let him do many of the things he wants to do. But the feelings of frustration that he expressed are commonly expressed by children. Their experience is that:

- children are treated differently from adults
- children's views usually have to give way to those of adults
- children are considered less capable than adults because they are small.

This handbook is intended as a practical guide for anyone working with young children – those under the age of eight – whether at home, in nursery, playgroup or school. It promotes the idea that children have a right to be involved in decisions that affect them.

Parents and childcare workers need to work together and share their ideas. The parents' leaflet which is published with the handbook is intended to support any discussion about how adults can help children to take responsibility and make decisions.

The basic principles that run through the handbook are:

- Children have a right to be treated with the same respect as adults.
- Children's feelings are as strong and valid as those of adults.
- Children know what is important to them and have the right to express their views and be listened to.
- Children's learning is active and relies on being given the opportunity to practice and develop their skills, knowledge and understanding. They will learn to participate by being given the opportunity to do so, starting with simple choices and moving on to more complex decisions as they become ready.

These principles apply to all children – regardless of their age, gender, race or ability.

It is not a simple issue.

What happens, for instance, if children decide after full and informed discussion that they want to drink cola at snack time rather than milk or fruit juice? Or that they want to use the computer to play 'zap' games rather than matching shapes?

The views of children will need to be balanced against those of others involved, and against such considerations as safety, health, finance and practicality. Their views will not necessarily prevail over those of adults – this handbook is about participation, not autonomy.

What is important – and should be every child's right – is that:

- adults give children the opportunity to express their views
- adults listen to what children say
- adults take children's views into account.

Benefits of involving young children

Research and anecdotal evidence show that, when the need or opportunity arises, children are capable of taking part in decision-making processes; can take responsibility for themselves and others; and can contribute usefully to family and community life.

When children are encouraged to participate in decisions that affect them the benefits can be far-reaching – for them, for adults and for society as a whole.

- Children learn to express their own needs, consider those of others, and develop skills of co-operation, negotiation and problem-solving.
- When their ideas and capabilities are respected, children's confidence and self-esteem grow.
- Participation develops children's sense that decisions are their own, and increases their commitment to making them work.
- Insights gained from children help adults to work more effectively and ensure that services provided are relevant to children's needs.

■ Children who are experienced participators are likely to go on to become capable and involved citizens, thus benefiting society as a whole.

Children's rights

Despite the feelings expressed by some people that children have too much freedom to do what they want, the reality for many is that they have very little say in decisions that affect them.

In legal terms, children are the responsibility of their parents and it is up to parents to decide whether to involve their children in important decisions such as where they live, which school they attend or what medical treatment they receive. Only when a child's family structure has broken down, and custody proceedings or care orders are in place, does the Children Act require local authorities and courts to consider a child's wishes and feelings when making decisions about their welfare.[1]

The right to participate is recognised in the *Convention on the Rights of the Child*, drawn up by the United Nations in 1989 and ratified by the UK. Article 12 argues that:

■ The governments of all countries should assure that a child who is capable of forming his or her own views should have the right to express those views freely in all matters affecting that child, and that the views of the child should be given due weight in accordance with the age and maturity of the child.

■ For this purpose, the child shall in particular be given the opportunity to be heard in all judicial and administrative proceedings affecting the child, either directly, or through a representative or an appropriate body, in a manner consistent with the procedural rules of national law.

For those brought up with the adage that children should be seen and not heard, this represents a major shift in thinking. Adults are used to making decisions for children 'in their best interests' because children – particularly young children – are assumed to be incapable of rational thought, to have little self-control and to be unable to consider the views of others.

Yet when children are given the opportunity to express their opinions, the results often confound these assumptions.

Children in a survey carried out in Liverpool 8 were asked:

'If we wanted to make a better place for children to live in, what would you like us to do?'

The children's top ten choices fell into two main categories: entertainment and leisure facilities (Camelot/Pleasure Island, roller dome etc) and social issues (less pollution, more houses and jobs, people to be nice).

The youngest children (7-8 years old) chose 'more zebra crossings' as their top preference.[2]

When considering what decisions we can entrust to children we have to make judgments about their capabilities. These judgments should be based on what we know of the individual children in our care, rather than on generalised views about children. All too often, such generalisations underestimate children's capacities and prevent children from showing us what they can achieve.

What do we mean by participation?

Participate	'have share, take part (in); have something of'
Consult	'have deliberations with' 'seek information or advice from' 'take into consideration (feelings, interests)'
Autonomy	'right of self government; personal freedom; freedom of the will' [*Concise Oxford Dictionary*]

At first sight there may not seem much difference between participation and consultation – both involve more than one party; both aim for some sort of exchange.

The main difference, as any of you who have been involved in consultation exercises will be aware, is that in **consultation** the people seeking your views will have the ultimate power. They decide what they will ask about, how they will ask it, the means by which views can be expressed, the time frame, and to what extent the views expressed will influence their decision.

Participation implies joint ownership of the decision-making process and active involvement of all parties. Power is shared.

In practice, any attempt to promote children's participation will involve consultation too. There are different levels of participation – and we need to be clear with ourselves and with children what level of participation we are offering.

The description that follows provides a framework for understanding the levels of participation. It is not assumed that early years workers will always aim for the 'highest' level of participation, but that they will choose the appropriate level for the child and the activity.

The framework was adapted by Roger Hart[3] from Arnstein's model of adult participation.[4]

Levels of participation

- **Manipulation** represents the lowest level of participation and is characterised by children doing or saying what adults wish them to do but with no real understanding of the issues. Children are asked what they think, adults use some of the ideas but give them no feedback on the influence those ideas have had on decisions that are made.
Example
Children are asked to make drawings of an ideal playground. Adults collect the ideas and produce a design for the playground but the children have no idea how their ideas were used and no analysis of the ideas suggested is undertaken.

- **Decoration** refers to situations where children are asked to take part in an event but not given any explanation of the issues or the reasons for their involvement.
Example
Children are asked to wear a T-shirt promoting an issue or to sing or dance at an event but have little idea of the purpose of the event and no say at all in its organisation.

- **Tokenism** is used to describe situations in which children are apparently given a voice but have little choice about the subject, the style of communicating it or any say in organising the occasion.
Example
Children are invited to sit on a panel at a conference with little or no substantive preparation on the subject and no consultation with the peers who, by implication, they represent.

- **Assigned but informed participation** requires that children understand the intentions of the project, know who made the decisions concerning their involvement and why, have a meaningful rather than a decorative role and that they volunteer to participate after the purpose of the project is made clear to them.
Example
At the World Summit for Children held in New York in 1990 a child was assigned to each of the 71 world leaders and fulfilled the role of ushering the leaders to the right places at the right times. This enabled the children to play a significant role as 'pages'. Had they been asked to speak their participation would merely have been tokenism as they were neither representative nor necessarily competent to speak on behalf of other children. But in the capacity in which they served they were enabled to make a valuable and appropriate contribution.

- Participation in which children are **consulted and informed** involves a process in which a project is designed and run by adults but children understand the process and their opinions are treated seriously.
Example
A survey conducted by an organisation to elicit children's views would invite the children to comment on, for example, television programmes or their experience of the environment. Draft proposals or a low cost version of a programme would be prepared and the same children asked again to comment. In this way the children are informed about the impact of their views on the proposals and are enabled to become involved in the process of developing those proposals.

- **Adult-initiated projects, sharing decisions with children**, are those which seek to involve children fully in the decision-making processes.
Example
An environment project to design a park for multi-purpose use involved a group of children and young people to develop the priorities and the design issues. The children produced a range of different models which were then exposed to local community members for comment and modification before being finalised.

- **Child-initiated and directed** projects are those where both the original idea and the implementation of that idea derive from children themselves.
Example
A group of children decide to develop a project to raise money for a charitable cause. They identify the charity, decide the strategy for raising money, organise the necessary activities, collect the money and send it to the charity.

- **Child-initiated projects, where there are shared decisions with adults** are those where the children identify or conceive the initial idea and then work with adults as equal partners in the project.

Example

A group of pupils are concerned about the levels of bullying in school. They form a coalition to petition the relevant authorities to take action to tackle the problem. As a result of their efforts, the school appoints peer counsellors to provide counselling, referral services, advice and information.

Different models of participation are appropriate for different settings. But examination of these approaches will provide a framework for understanding the ways in which children can be encouraged and enabled to take greater responsibility for policies, services and projects which affect their lives.

Participation in practice

Children control their own pain relief

At Great Ormond Street Children's Hospital children were given the opportunity to decide how much medication they took to control their own pain.

Safety procedures were built in so that the amount of drug available was never more than the maximum recommended dose. Doctors found that the amounts children took were similar to or less than they would have prescribed.

The children were, safely, able to control their own pain relief.[5]

Children as health educators

In over 70 countries throughout the world children are taking part in programmes to improve their own health and that of others in their community.

The original Child-to-Child concept was to give health information to older children who were caring for younger sisters and brothers. This proved so successful that now children are passing on what they know to their families, schools and the wider community.

Hygiene, nutrition and safety are the focus of many of these programmes, with additional topics being developed appropriate to each community's needs – such as land conservation and the creation of vegetable gardens.

The children are actively involved in finding out the information they need and in passing it on to others. They use a range of methods to get their message across – plays and puppet shows; stories and songs; posters and quizzes. [6]

Children as carers

Thousands of children in the UK – 40,000 is the latest estimate – are caring for a sick or disabled relative. They perform the same tasks as adult carers do – feeding, dressing, bathing and toileting. Some of these carers are as young as three years old. Many get no help from social services or health professionals. Because they are under 18 and have the legal status of children they do not receive social services benefits or have access to statutory services and support. Many are afraid to talk to professionals for fear that they themselves – if believed – might be taken into care. Like adult carers, most children want to continue caring, but with support. [7]

Children help to get funding for their group

In Kirkcaldy, Fife, the Victoria Community After School Children's Club has been running for two years with the help of funding from BBC Scotland Children in Need.

The group have been developing a participative approach during this time: the children drew up their own rules for the club, are involved in planning activities and, increasingly, take care of each other.

The children's ownership of the club has paid off in many ways. They keep the rules they made; it is the children, rather than the workers, who remind each other to put on seatbelts in the minibus – and 'we didn't get banned from anywhere this summer!'

Having successfully involved the children in planning and budgeting for activities, the workers wanted the children to take part in applying for funding for the next year.

The children, aged five to 10, produced a story book in the shape of a minibus, describing in words and pictures what the club meant to them. Every child's picture or story was included. They also made a quilt featuring drawings and photographs of their activities, a year's project. The names of all the children and workers involved in the club are visible on the quilt.

The book and a photo of the quilt formed part of the club's funding application, which the children presented to the Scottish co-ordinator of BBC Children in Need. Their application was successful and the quilt was shown on television.

How to use this handbook

Section 1: Where do we start from?

This gives adults the opportunity to explore their own beliefs about children and childhood. It will give some idea of the implications for adults of promoting children's right to make decisions and take responsibility. It looks at:

- the barriers that might prevent children from participating
- why it is important for children to make decisions and take responsibility
- what this might look like in practice.

What we believe about children's capabilities affects the opportunities we offer to them and their response to us. If children are to participate successfully we may need to reconsider our approach to them – both in the way we relate to them personally and professionally and in the way that society as a whole views and treats them. We need to explore which differences between children and adults are real and which are based on myth and stereotype. Where we do find difference we need to welcome and work positively with it, rather than assuming that difference must imply inequality.

Section 2: How are children participating now?

This encourages you to look at your current practice. It contains questions that can be used to monitor to what extent the children you care for are now able to make decisions and take responsibility, and suggests general approaches that might facilitate further participation.

Section 3: Participation – how to do it

This describes a range of methods that can be used to find out what is important to children. Most of them have been tested in early years groups and stories of their experiences appear throughout the handbook.

Simply asking young children what they think is unlikely to work.

- Some children will not understand the question or why you are asking it.
- Some may be more interested in pleasing you than in expressing what they feel, and will try to guess what answer you want to hear.
- Some children will not be able to express themselves verbally – so the techniques include visual methods, movement and gesture, as well as the use of stories, drama and dialogue.

Some young children have difficulty identifying or expressing their feelings – or lack the confidence to do so – so this section includes activities to develop self-esteem and self-expression.

Techniques are suggested for exploring group issues such as setting and maintaining rules, resolving conflicts, solving problems and making decisions.

Some techniques call for particular skills which may be related to the children's age or previous experience. For instance, being able to make representational drawings; being able to work in a group, taking turns, co-operating with others; being able to use words and symbols.

To help you decide if a particular technique is suitable for the children you are working with, there is a guide to suggest the age range which is likely to be most appropriate.

All over the world throughout history, those in power have tended to regard those over whom they have power as inferior, less human. Rulers have believed that those whom they oppress are of less value and have different – and fewer – needs and feelings. They have denied basic human rights to peasants, slaves, women and lunatics, and to people of a race, religion, culture or sexuality other than that which dominates. They have even taken their lives.

What, you may wonder, does this have to do with children?

Consider some of the ways in which children are viewed and treated, now, in this society.

- A teacher puts sticky tape over the mouth of a four year old boy who will not stop singing nursery rhymes when she asks him to. News of this hits the headlines for a day or two. We are told that the school has apologised to the boy's parents. No mention is made of anyone apologising to the boy.
- Charters set out our rights in relation to public and erstwhile public bodies. The charter dealing with schools is a 'Parent's Charter' – it addresses itself to the rights of adults rather than the rights of children.
- Children are the smallest and most vulnerable members of our society. They are legally protected from dangers such as alcohol, amusement arcades and even paid employment. Hitting an adult would be deemed to be an assault. Yet parents are allowed to hit their children – provided they don't go 'too far' – and in law this is called 'reasonable chastisement'.
- Some religious leaders – not all – justify carrying out circumcision of baby boys without anaesthetic on the grounds that they are too young to feel pain as we know it.

The messages given here are that children are viewed and treated differently from adults: their feelings and opinions either do not count, or count for less, than those of adults.

Attitudes to children

As a society, we have an ambivalent attitude to children.

On one hand we adopt a sentimental approach, portraying children as cute and innocent, calling them 'little angels' and claiming that they can do no wrong.

On the other hand, we portray them as wild, cruel and selfish, refer to them as animals, call them 'little devils' and act as though we still believe in the doctrine of original sin: that children are born bad and must be made good. No sentimentality here; children are something to be afraid of, constrained, even – surreptitiously – hated.

Press reporting of the murder of James Bulger epitomised these attitudes: the innocence of the murdered two year old was contrasted with the demonic nature of the two 10 year olds who killed him, children who 'had the faces of normal boys but hearts of unparalleled evil' (Daily Mirror).

Such extreme and contradictory views of children influence the way we treat them and obscure a more simple truth: children are neither little angels nor little devils – they are people. People with as wide a range of behaviours, feelings and characteristics as that other group of people which we call adults.

Despite this, we act as though the differences between children and adults are greater than the similarities. We say that there are characteristics specific to children and that we can generalise these.

Generalisations

Consider some of the things that are said about children:

'You can't reason with children; they don't understand.'
'Children have no self-control ... give them an inch and they'll take a mile.'
'Children are egocentric ... irresponsible ... a nuisance .... cruel.'

Now ask yourself:

- Are all children like this?
- Are any adults like this?

Is the generalisation 'Children are cruel' any more true or helpful than 'Adults are kind'?

The differences between children and adults are not as absolute as these generalisations imply. Some children behave in ways that are considered 'adult' and some adults behave in ways considered to be 'childish'. Most of us stray between the two, depending on how we are feeling, who we are with and how we are being treated.

Turning into stereotypes

The trouble with generalisations is that they can easily become stereotypes which we expect all children to fit into. When children act in ways that do not fit our stereotypes, we respond in one of several ways:

■ *We fail to recognise their capability*

When a child of four makes her own way home from nursery after becoming separated from her mother, we tend to say how lucky she was to get home safely. We are less likely to acknowledge her navigational skills, ability to use pedestrian crossings and other aids to cross busy roads and her general confidence and independence.

■ *We grant them honorary adult status*

A child who displays 'adult' characteristics such as independence or the ability to consider another person's point of view may be told how 'grown-up' or 'mature' he is.

■ *We feel threatened*

A child who is able to reason, and attempts to do so, may be called cheeky or insolent or told 'not to answer back'.

■ *We consider what they are doing to be unsuitable*

Where a child takes responsibility for others – caring for a younger sibling or a parent who is sick – we say she is being deprived of her childhood. We have a similar response to children who work and contribute to the income of their family.

What we rarely do is question the stereotypes. For most adults it seems more comfortable to continue thinking of children as dependent, immature and powerless and to expect them to behave in a 'childish' manner.

That, after all, is how most adults were treated when they were children – it is all part of 'normal' childhood.

Or is it?

What is childhood?

We tend to view childhood as a fixed period of life that is natural, universal and unchanging. We imbue it with romanticised notions of happiness, innocence and freedom from responsibility. We cannot imagine a change in the status of children that would not threaten childhood itself. And yet this long period of childhood that we consider so natural and right is a relatively recent way of thinking, and one which is found only in rich industrialised societies.

Another view of childhood

All over the world children play an important role within their families and communities, helping with domestic work, taking care of younger children and contributing to their families' income and welfare from an early age. It is estimated that between 100 and 230 million children between the ages of four and 15 are working worldwide – the majority of them with their families in agricultural work, textiles and selling.

■ In Bangladesh, seven year old Suma and six year old Shepali rise early to collect flowers which they make into garlands and sell in the busy squares and crossroads of Dhaka city. By 10am they have sold them all and are free to go to school. In the afternoon they play before going in search of more flowers to sell into the evening.

■ Eight year old Jamil also works in Dhaka, helping out on a minibus from eight in the morning till six at night. He enjoys seeing different places in the city. After work he attends night-school. It's his ambition to drive a bus and earn a lot of money for his mother.[8]

There is great international concern about children being exploited as cheap labour, missing out on school and play, and working in conditions that threaten their health and development. These are often valid concerns; however, in other cases children work without damaging their health or educational prospects. Many children need to work because of poverty. To us in the 'West' with our idealised view of a carefree childhood, this seems shocking. But what has surprised many of those seeking to prevent child exploitation, is that many children choose to work: they want to make their contribution. And for many children there are positive aspects to their work; they learn skills that help prepare them for adult life and, as well as earning an income, they command respect in their families.

The beginning of childhood

Home life

Not so long ago in this country the majority of children were working and taking their place alongside adults.

In medieval society the idea of childhood as we know it did not exist. This was before the time when children came to be seen as having an innocence that needed to be protected. As soon as they were weaned, could walk and talk, children were regarded as little adults. They ate, drank and dressed as their parents did. Children and adults played the same games. Children were included in sexual talk, songs and games.

Most children worked alongside their parents: tending crops and animals, spinning, weaving or in other work carried out – as work then was – around the home. Some children would be apprenticed to work away from home.

New ideas which affected the way in which children were regarded, and the concept of childhood itself, came about in the seventeenth century. Religious reformers, led by the Puritans in England and the Jesuits in France, promoted a more sober, godly and moral approach to life. Linked to this, a new view of childhood was being formed. This had two strands: childhood as a time of innocence; childhood as a time of weakness. To protect the innocence, children needed to be separated from many of the adult ways which might otherwise corrupt them. To strengthen the weakness, children's character and reason was to be developed through instruction and discipline. The best known Jesuit saying demonstrates their confidence in the effectiveness of their philosophy: 'Give me a child for the first seven years and you may do what you like with him afterwards'.[9]

Play time

This new concept of childhood – of a separation between children and adults – can be traced in the development of clothes, games and books. Like many developments, however, it was confined to the 'upper' classes and it was several hundred years before the lives of working people were affected.

Pictures of the time show that, while girls continued to be dressed in small versions of their mothers' clothes, special garments for boys were beginning to appear.

Games that had been played by people of all ages and classes were abandoned by some adults as 'children's games'. The same thing happened with toys which people of all ages had previously played with, such as dolls, whipping tops and windmills.

When children were regarded as little adults they had worked using adult tools; now they were to be given miniaturised versions of adult tools to play with and learn from. Educational toys specifically for children were introduced. Maria Edgeworth, in her *Essays on Practical Education* published in 1789, describes the 'rational toyshop' stocked with items such as:

'sturdy carts, small gardening tools, printing presses, looms and furniture which takes to pieces and reassembles .. pencils, scissors, paste, tools and workbenches'.[10]

The separation of child from adult can also be traced in books. Students used to be offered classical texts in full, unexpurgated form. Now they were rewritten for children, appearing under titles such as *Comedies of Terence made very decent while changing very little*.

Books of etiquette aimed at children began to appear, with the aim of 'polishing their minds and manners'. This concern with children's moral welfare grew during the eighteenth century, as books began to appear advising parents on how to bring up their children.[11]

Working life

The majority of children, however, were still working. For them the Industrial Revolution, which began during the eighteenth century, brought more changes.

Home and work began to be separated. Work that had previously been carried out manually at home was transferred to factories and mills which used machinery powered by water or steam. At first children followed their parents into the mines, mills and factories to work, but conditions were dangerous, unhealthy and exhausting and while it was considered acceptable to expose working men to these dangers, women and children were seen as more vulnerable. Laws were gradually introduced to limit the number of hours that women and children could work and to raise the age at which children could start to work. These laws applied only to factories, workshops and mines – many children continued to be employed in other work. Even as recently as the 1900s an investigation into child labour in London found that around a quarter of children aged between 5 and 13 had paid jobs outside school hours.[12]

School life

Mediaeval schools, where they existed, were for training clerks of all ages. Age was not an important consideration. Learning was by rote and students moved on to the next class when they had memorised what was being taught, not just because they were a year older.

An industrialised and increasingly bureaucratic society needs a workforce that is literate and numerate. That was one reason for the widespread increase in schools at the end of the nineteenth century. Another was worry about the safety, health and morals of children in the towns who could no longer be employed and spent much of the time fending for themselves on the streets while their mothers were working. Schools were needed to keep children off the streets and teach them the 3Rs, their place in life and moral values.

It was some time before going to school became part of childhood for all children. The early schools were fee-paying and families had also to manage without any earnings the children might have had. Successive Acts of Parliament attempted to make attendance at school compulsory and to prevent the employment of children. Many of these were initially unsuccessful, as you can see from the summary of this legislation on page 71.

A better childhood?

Childhood, as we have seen, has changed and lengthened. It is not changes in children that have brought this about, but changes in our society.

In many ways, children's lives have improved: they no longer work down mines or up chimneys; few die in infancy and all receive health care and schooling. Materially, the lives of many children in this country have improved considerably: they have more toys, equipment and possessions than children have ever had. Nevertheless, poverty is a reality for a growing number of children.

With these changes, however, has come a growing dependence of children on their parents, not only for their upkeep, but also for other aspects of their lives such as their mobility. In 1971, 80% of children made their own way to school. By 1990 only 9% were

doing so. Road building programmes have enabled cars to proliferate and become capable of greater speeds. Parents no longer feel that it is safe for children to travel alone, so many more are taken to school, often in cars. Paradoxically, this means an even greater increase in road traffic. It also means that children become less capable of travelling safely on their own as they get less opportunity to practise the necessary skills. [13]

Just as the change in children's mobility is caused by an increase in road traffic, so many of the other changes in the way we perceive children and childhood stem, not from anything intrinsic to children, but from religious, scientific, economic, social and political developments within our society. It is adults who have decided what childhood should consist of and how long it should last, and they have done this with very little reference to children themselves.

Many children do not share adults' romantic view of childhood as a carefree time. What adults see as freedom from responsibility, children often feel as powerlessness. Talk to children, and one of the main reasons that they give for wanting to grow up is so that they can have more control over their lives.

From what we know of children in other parts of the world and in other times, childhood does not have to be a prolonged time of dependence and marginalisation from society. Children are capable of contributing much; many are doing so now in this society as we can see, for instance, in the number of children who have taken on the role of carer for members of their family. We need to recognise their capabilities, acknowledge their right to participate and enable them to do so.

Why is it an insult to be childish?

We regard children as being different from adults. Many adults go one step further and regard children as being inferior to adults.

- Have you ever wondered why so many words that describe children have come to be used as insults? *childish infantile immature puerile babyish cry baby you're acting like a two year old*
- All people under the age of 18 are 'legal minors'. The word 'minor' means 'lesser of two things'. When we place less value on a group of people, we also place less value on their feelings and opinions.

Adults don't treat children differently just because they are small; children are also likely to be less informed and experienced than adults. But size can determine how people are treated, as John Holt

illustrates in his book *Escape from Childhood*.
A woman was amongst a crowd of people surging into a New York department store at sale time. Ahead of her were two small boys whose heads came just above her waist. Feeling affectionate and mischievous, she put a finger tip on the top of each boy's head and walked like that for a step or two. But only a step or two, for two furious adult faces looked up at her and one of them said 'What the hell do you think you are doing?' The two 'boys' were midgets.[14]

Behind the woman's act, and the laughter of those to whom she told her story, was this thought – that if the midgets* really had been children it would have been all right to walk along with her fingers on their heads.

* Some people prefer the term 'people of restricted growth'.

The abuse of power over children

Some adults abuse the power they have over children – and justify their use of punishment and coercion as being a necessary part of child-rearing.

Children can be hurt and humiliated, by loving adults, 'for their own good'. To add insult to injury, they may even be told: 'It didn't really hurt' or 'This hurts me more than it hurts you' or 'You'll thank me for this later'.

Few people will intervene if they see a child being hit by his parents, possibly because they don't feel confident about doing so. A child 'belongs to' his parents and they are seen as having a right to discipline him as they see fit. (There are parallels here with the relationship of ownership that husbands used to claim over their wives, which allowed abuse to take place, without intervention, as it was a 'domestic dispute'.)

A number of people saw James Bulger being led away crying to what we now know was his death, but no one intervened. Is it so surprising? We are used to seeing children in shopping malls and other places being threatened, slapped and dragged along. We are used to seeing their tears, hearing them cry, and doing nothing. The only difference here was that this little child was with two bigger children rather than with an adult. With hindsight we know that his death could have been avoided if only someone had intervened.

'Children should be seen and not heard'

Another way in which we demonstrate our inferior regard for children is in our reluctance to listen to them and to take their feelings and opinions into account.

Adults make decisions that affect every aspect of children's lives. Some might be considered of minor importance, like what children wear. But think how we would feel if we were told what to wear. Decisions are made about who they can play with, what they are taught, where they live and with whom. Rarely do we ask them: 'What do you think? How do you feel? What would you like?' When they do try to tell us they may find that they are ignored, disbelieved, even ridiculed.

In a UK consultation with five to 18 year olds, the Children's Rights Development Unit found children consistently complained that they had not been adequately listened to when families made major decisions. They frequently mentioned issues, such as moving house and divorce, on which they would have liked to have been given an opportunity to express their views and have them taken seriously.

Sometimes children are not even seen, let alone heard. In planning and policy-making children are often invisible – their needs or the impact on them of proposed changes are rarely taken into account. One example of this is environmental planning, where housing developments are designed without asking children for their views. The result may be an environment that is unfriendly to children, has no space in which they can safely play and socialise, and which exposes them to dangers of poor design and dangerous traffic flows. When children are given the opportunity to participate in such planning their contribution is valuable, as the case study on page 35 shows.

'Adults know best'

Children are often told that they are too young to know, or that their views do not count; that adults have far more experience than children and know what is best.

The first thing to be said here is that, though they do not know as much about the world as most adults, children do know how *they* feel and what is important to *them*.

Secondly, while adults may have more experience than children, there is still no clear consensus amongst adults as to the best way of bringing up children. Consider the mass of advice and guidance, much of it contradictory, offered to parents in childcare manuals over the years. We are still arguing about how best to educate children, what forms of discipline are effective, how to 'instil moral values'. We are not even sure what is the best family structure in which to raise children.

Even where adults do agree on what is best for children, we often fail to provide it.

- We know that there are links between poverty and ill health and low educational achievement. Yet one in three children in the UK now lives in poverty – a threefold rise over the last 16 years.
- We know that thousands of children are abused by those whom they love and trust, yet most of our endeavours go into warning them of the dangers posed by strangers.
- We know that children are becoming increasingly unfit and one reason for this is lack of physical exercise. Yet schools are urged to sell off their playing fields; sport has a low priority within the National Curriculum; and over and over and over again adults tell children not to run.
- We know that most children suffer when their parents separate, but the divorce rate continues to rise.
- It is adults who wage wars, plant land mines, pollute the environment and stockpile or destroy food in Europe and the US to safeguard prices while millions of people throughout the world go hungry.

If this is our best, it is not good enough.

We must begin to consider the impact on children of our policies and actions. We must seek their views, listen to what they say and enable them to participate in creating a more peaceful and equitable world.

Why it is important for children to participate

Children have a right to participate in decisions that affect them. They know what is important to them and will have to live with the consequences of any decisions made.

Benefits for children

- Participation offers children the opportunity to express and understand their own feelings and needs. Only when they are able to do this can they consider the feelings and needs of others.
- Participation helps children to develop the skills of communication, debate, negotiation and compromise and so to achieve a balance between their own needs and those of others.
- Through participation children gain information that helps them to understand both possibilities, and constraints such as budget limitations and

safety considerations.
- By choosing among various options, children develop the skill of decision-making, both individually and as part of a group.
- When children's ideas, feelings and capabilities are treated with respect, their confidence and self-esteem grow.

Benefits for parents

Parents who involve their children in decision-making find that:

- when they involve their children – asking them for their opinion, listening to what they say and taking their views into account – their relationship with their children becomes much easier;
- there is far less conflict and much more co-operation between them and their children;
- their children respond positively to being treated with respect and, in turn, treat their parents with more respect.

After she attended a parenting group, one parent from the Langley Children's project, Middleton, wrote:
I decided to attend Parent-Link to make the job of bringing up my seven year old son and the children of other working parents an easier task ... Parent-Link taught me how to involve children with decision making, how to help them in expressing their own opinions, and bring about co-operation between parents/carers/workers and children.

The sessions on listening to children and being listened to in return, and acknowledging, expressing and – more importantly – accepting feelings on both sides were especially helpful to me ...

I thoroughly enjoyed the course and would encourage others to attend.

My final thought: **give respect to children and you will earn respect yourselves.**

Benefits for the group

- Participation increases children's sense of ownership of, and responsibility for, their environment, activities and rules. They are more likely to co-operate with, and support, provision which they have helped to shape.
- Insights gained from children can help adults to work more effectively.
- Participation ensures that services provided are relevant to, and meet the needs of, the children using them and can adapt to reflect changing needs.
- Provision that meets the needs of those who use it

will be popular and likely to survive.

Benefits for society

- Early experience of participation in decisions that affect them helps children gain the skills, knowledge and understanding that can then be used to participate in the wider society. Society benefits from the input of more capable and involved citizens.
- Promoting participatory practice encourages democratic procedures and respect for the principles and practice of democratic life.

Barriers to participation

What are the barriers that may prevent successful participation by children? What are the implications for adults of trying to overcome these?

Attitudes

The main barrier which prevents children from having the opportunity to make decisions is the widespread belief that they are not capable of making informed decisions and that adults know best.

Anyone promoting participation will need to be clear in their own mind how they will respond to the familiar argument that children cannot be given responsibility or take decisions because they are inexperienced, irrational, do not know enough. Earlier parts of this section which explore attitudes to children and examples of their capabilities might help here, as might the discussion on expectations of children which follows.

Expectations of children

What we expect of children has an effect on how well their capacities will develop.

Low expectations based on the stereotypical view of children as being irrational, irresponsible and selfish may affect the opportunities that we offer to children. As a result, children may not have the chance to show us how capable they are, or develop their capability to make decisions, take responsibility and care for others.

Expectations will also influence children's actual achievement: children will live up – or down – to our expectations of them. Evidence of this was shown in research, known variously as 'Pygmalion in the Classroom' and 'The Self-fulfilling Prophecy', which was carried out in the US during the 1960s and

confirmed by a number of other studies.

The self-fulfilling prophecy

Researchers wanted to find out what effect, if any, the expectations of teachers had on children's academic performance.

Children were tested to find out their IQ level. The researchers then assigned random IQ scores to these children, that is to say, scores that were not related to their actual tested scores. The children were not told what these scores were. The teachers were given the random scores which they believed reflected each individual child's actual IQ.

- Teachers made greater efforts with those children whom they believed to have a high IQ. If such a child failed to understand something, the teacher would repeat the explanation, or try another, until the child had grasped the concept. The teachers were proceeding on the assumption that this child should be able to understand and that if he had not done so, their own explanation must be at fault, not the child's understanding.
- Teachers made far less effort with children they believed to have a low IQ. If such a child failed to grasp a concept, the teachers did not persevere. They assumed that the concept must be beyond the child's grasp and to try another explanation would be a waste of time and put undue pressure on the child. Here, the teachers were proceeding on the basis that it was the child's understanding that was at fault, not their explanation.

The children who the teachers believed had high IQ levels achieved far more than those who were believed to have low IQ levels – regardless of their actual IQ. The children's achievements were not related to what they were theoretically capable of achieving, but to what was expected of them.

When adults believe children to be capable of something, children are more likely to become capable of it.

- They are given the opportunity to succeed and the necessary support .
- They achieve success.
- Their confidence and self-esteem grows.
- They adopt a 'can do' rather than a 'can't do' approach.

Children who do not want to take part

Some children do not want to be involved in making decisions and do not want to take responsibility. There may be children who do not want to be involved in some participatory methods; children who do not want to join in Circle Time, for instance.

There are a number of possible reasons.

■ *Some children are not happy in a large group*

Perhaps such times have been used previously to control them or to pressure them to perform in a particular way. Where this is the case we must respect children's right not to be involved and look at ways in which we can make such participatory methods more engaging and enjoyable for them.

■ *Some children have no experience of making choices*

They may be 'lost' when presented with choice and seem to need adult direction. For these children, choice needs to be introduced gradually, starting with simple choices between given options and building on the children's confidence in their own ability.

■ *Children may lack belief in their own abilities*

Children who have frequently been told that they are stupid, or careless, or lazy, may begin to believe these things of themselves and either act accordingly or not attempt new things for fear of failing.

■ *Some children may lack self-esteem*

They may have become dependent on adults for praise or encouragement and are not able to evaluate for themselves their own strengths and weaknesses.

If children are to participate successfully they need to feel good about themselves, their skills and qualities and to be able to recognise and appreciate these attributes in others.

The development of self-esteem is an essential part of the process of promoting children's participation. Daily activities and experiences within the group need to build on what children can do and reinforce their awareness of their capabilities.

Some activities to develop self-esteem can be found in Section 3.

Information

In order to participate in decision-making children need information about the decision-making process itself and about the issues that are to be decided.

One of the barriers to children's participation is that they are dependent on adults for much of the information they receive, whether directly through adults showing and telling them things or indirectly through adult control over their access to other information networks such as the television.

It is all too easy to take it for granted that everyone else knows whatever we know. We need to remember what it feels like to be the 'outsider' in our dealings with other adults: in meetings, for instance, when we feel excluded by the use of jargon and sets of initials that we are not familiar with, or when we do not know the procedure for getting something done.

If this is what it feels like for adults, think how much more so it must feel for children, for whom everything is new, has to be learnt about, worked out and made sense of.

If children are to make informed decisions, adults need to consider carefully what information they will need and how this can be presented in ways that are engaging and meaningful.

We cannot rely just on telling children things. They need:

■ to see things demonstrated
■ to handle information in as concrete a form as possible
■ to experience things at first hand.

It can be helpful to look at the methods that children use when they present information to others, as in the Child-to-Child projects, where they used a range of methods including puppets, plays, stories, songs, posters and games (see page 8 above).

Whatever methods are used, children will need time to assimilate the information and opportunity to use and test it – to fully understand and make it their own.

How things work

No-one can participate unless they know how the 'system' works. You need to make sure that children know how your system works before you can expect them to participate in it.

■ *The people in your setting*

Children need to be told who does what, and what their roles are. There is no point, for instance, in having a school counsellor to help children with personal problems if the children do not know what she is there for or how they can get to see her. If playgroups operate a parent rota, do all the children understand that the parent on duty is there to help all the children, not just their own child? (An exercise to explore children's perception of adult roles is described in Section 3.)

■ *The structure of power within your setting*

Children need to know, first, that decisions are made – some children may think things 'just happen'. They need to know what decisions can be taken, by whom, and that some decisions can be made 'on the spot' and others have to be discussed in meetings. They need to understand that some decisions everyone will agree with, some matters will be decided by a majority vote; other decisions will be imposed from 'outside' by funders or registering authorities and even if no one agrees with them they still have to be carried out.

■ *Which decisions they can participate in, how, and to what extent*
If a group decision is to be made, will the whole group have to agree or will there be a vote? If there is a vote, do those in the minority understand that they will not get what they voted for? Will the children decide what is to happen, or are you asking for their views before you decide?

■ *What influence they will have on the outcome*
If participation is to be a positive experience for children, adults must be clear about the extent to which children's views will prevail. If we ask for their views and then disregard them children will get the following messages:
  – that they are not being listened to or taken seriously;
  – that their views are wrong;
  – that this is a token exercise – more hoops to jump through.
None of these messages will encourage future participation.

■ *What else has to be taken into account*
Children also need to know what factors other than personal preference we take into account when making decisions. This could be health and safety, cost, time, space, equipment and the implications for other people.

These are complex issues and will have to be approached a bit at a time.

(Techniques for involving children in decision-making can be found in Section 3).

Access

In a world built for adults many things are physically out of reach to a young child. Wherever possible, the environment needs to be adapted and laid out in such a way that children can see what is available and help themselves to what they need. It is hard,

for instance, for a child to choose her own activities if she has to depend on an adult to tell her what is available and to reach it for her.

Children are dependent on adults for their wider mobility, so if children are to be involved in meetings outside of your setting, or out of usual hours, they will need to be transported and escorted. This may have extra cost implications.

Another barrier to participation will be finding out the views of children with limited or no speech. Here we will need to use other methods involving physical movement and gesture – a nod or shake of the head, thumbs up or down, asking children to point or move to their preferred option. Section 3 has a number of simple, practical suggestions.

Resources

■ *Financial cost*
Some of the techniques require resources that groups may not have, or whose use is limited by finance, such as camera film. Most of the materials, however, will be generally available in early years settings and should not present any problems.

■ *Staff time*
Staff already spend time in planning and preparing for curriculum activities and making visual aids and other equipment. Where participation is an integral part of the curriculum, rather than something that is added on, planning and preparation do not demand significant extra staff time. However, you will need to prepare background information if the children are to make informed decisions.

More time will be needed when children are involved in decisions currently being made by one or two adults. It also takes longer to reach decisions in larger meetings, where everyone has their say, and when the experience is a new one for people and there is much that needs to be explained.

■ *Speed*
It is often quicker to do things for children than to let them do things for themselves. But just as we recognise the need – say – to allow the time for a one year old to feed herself, because we know this is a skill that she needs to acquire and that she will only acquire it through practice, so we need to allow the time for children to acquire, through practice, the skill of decision-making.

■ *Waste*

One concern is that resources, whether of time or materials, may be wasted if children make decisions that turn out to be wrong, or not to work. This should be no reason to deny children the right to participate; we have all made mistakes and, provided that we have a chance to acknowledge and evaluate them, we usually learn from them. Part of our role as responsible adults will be to decide what risks can be taken without jeopardising children's safety and welfare, or the funding of our group.

Managing participation in a group

One concern that people have is how to balance the wishes of one child against the wishes of others in the group. What do you do if three children on an outing want to do three completely different things?

Participation does not necessarily mean that all children will be able to do what they want. It does mean that they will be given information and involved in deciding what they, as a group, will do.

In the situation above:

■ Discuss the outing with the children beforehand. Let them know what the options will be and find out what they most want to do.

■ Plan the outing so that each child knows she will be able to do at least one of the things she wants. If necessary, remind her that if she is to have her wish (or 'turn') so must the other children. That is fair.

■ Remind the children of time limits and talk with them if, for any reason, plans have to change.

For instance, a boat trip has been promised, but one child becomes involved in a story-telling session and wants to stay for the next story. Let him know that there will not be time to do both – he must choose between another story and going on a boat.

Very young children will not be able to take part in planning like this – they are spontaneous and respond to stimuli in their immediate presence. This means that they may not know what they want till they see it.

You will need to make sure they get frequent opportunities to do what they want – they cannot wait long for their 'turn' – and then occupy them in other ways (singing songs, having a drink, exploring the contents of your bag ...) while other children have their turn.

New ways of doing things

We get used to doing things in a particular way and find it hard to imagine how they could be done differently. We may also feel that our way works well and that change will be unsettling, even threatening, to us.

Involving children is going to mean change for most of us. The formal meetings that we have, with minutes, agendas and reports, are unlikely to engage children – let us be honest, they are not always that exciting for adults either. If children are to participate, we need to find ways of involving them that they enjoy and feel comfortable with.

Power sharing

However convinced we are of children's right to participate, we may find it hard, in practice, to give up some of the power that we currently hold – particularly if power over children is the only power we feel that we possess in this society. We may want children to be involved only in so far as they agree with us and find it hard when they question or challenge principles and practice that we hold dear.

What happens, for instance, if children decide after full and informed discussion that they want to drink cola at snack time rather than milk or fruit juice? Or that they want to use the computer to play 'zap' games rather than matching shapes?

One approach to this is to ask: 'What happens if adults, after full and informed discussion, want to drink cola or play 'zap' games? Would you try to stop them for their own good?'

A second approach is to think: 'Children are at a formative stage. We have a responsibility for their healthy growth and should not offer them drinks containing a lot of sugar, or games that condone violence.'

With this approach we need to acknowledge that what is forbidden can be very tempting and that peer pressure and advertising are strong forces. We will not be able to stop children forever from trying these things, but we can give them some space in which to develop healthier tastes and less violent pursuits.

You will have to decide where you stand on issues such as these, tell children why you think as you do – and make sure your own behaviour reflects your beliefs.

We need to examine our motives in promoting participation carefully.

■ Are we really prepared to share power with

children or do we want them to endorse our power?

■ Which issues are negotiable and which are not?

Communicating with parents

Other adults may also feel threatened when children exercise the right to participate. Children whose parents encourage them to question, challenge and share in decision-making may find that teachers resist their attempts to do the same thing in school. Conversely, early years settings that encourage children to participate may meet resistance from parents.

A parents' leaflet is available to complement *Never too young* to support groups which want to work together with parents in adopting a participative approach.

What does participation look like in practice?

The process of promoting children's participation will be a gradual one and will need to take into account:

■ each child's experience, knowledge, skills and understanding

■ the ability of the child to express her needs and to balance these against the needs of others.

It will start with:

■ listening carefully to children

■ treating what they say with respect

■ encouraging them to feel that their views are important and that they do have a right to be involved in decisions that affect them.

A large part of the process will involve building on children's existing capacities by providing information; giving them opportunities to practise skills, exercise choice and take responsibility; and respecting the rights of those who don't yet want to do so.

It will mean looking at decisions that affect children and asking ourselves:

■ Is this something the children could decide on?

■ How can we involve them?

■ What might the consequences be for them, for us and our group?

Participation will not mean suddenly giving over all power and responsibility to young children. This would be unrealistic; most children – unused to having a say in even the small details of their lives – would be unprepared and ill-equipped for this.

It would also be irresponsible: young children do need the help of adults to set boundaries, to alert them to danger and to ensure that their need for food, warmth, sleep, love, protection, education and play are met.

■ *Children under four*

A realistic model of participation for children under the age of four might be that they choose, from given options, the food they eat, the clothes they wear, the activities they engage in, the friends they play with and the group they attend.

■ *Children from four to eight*

For children between four and eight, participation might extend to helping to resolve conflict; being involved in setting and maintaining rules; caring for others; suggesting additional activities, menus, equipment, and possible changes to their physical environment and the routines of their day.

(These age ranges are given as a guide only – see pages 24 for guidance on how to judge children's capacity and what we can expect of children at different ages).

What might happen – assessing the risks

As adults responsible for the welfare of young children, we need to decide what decisions they can take and which we should take for them.

How do we do this?

First we need to consider the possible consequences of a decision, both on the child herself and on others:

■ What risks might she be taking?

■ Are they risks it would be reasonable for her to take?

■ How well can she cope with them?

■ What might she learn from the experience?

■ If we don't give her the opportunity to experience these things within the relative safety, watchfulness and support of our settings, when and how will she experience them?

At home

A baby climbs on to a low wooden table. An adult is close by. The baby starts to crawl, forwards and backwards, over the surface of the table. When crawling backwards she stops as soon as she feels the edge of the table on her shin, turns her head, looks at the edge and moves away from it. After half an hour she has finished exploring the table, the new vantage point that it offers and the boundaries of her body. She crawls backwards to the edge and lowers herself gently to the floor.

The risk for this child was that she might fall and hurt herself. She showed that she could safely handle this risk on her own.

At playgroup

Outside there is snow on the ground. Inside, the hall is well heated and a group of children who have been chasing each other are hot. They ask if they can take their jumpers off. The playgroup worker says they can.

One child starts to pull his T shirt off too. The playgroup worker tells him she thinks it is too cold for that. He says he is still too hot. She acknowledges that he is now, but should cool down now that his jumper is off. If he is still hot later he can take the T shirt off. Fifteen minutes later she sees him pulling his T shirt off and, forgetting what she had said, asks him not to. He reminds her: 'But you said I could take it off later if I'm still hot!' She tells him he is right, apologises and he takes it off. Ten minutes later they are reading a story together and he is snuggling into her, which is unusual for him. She asks if she can feel how warm he is. His skin is cool. She tells him she thinks it is time to put his T shirt back on and explains why. He does.

The risk for this child is that he might get a cold and, having asthma, he needs to avoid this complication where possible. The playgroup worker is not sure that he will think to put his T shirt on if he cools down – though he did make the opposite connection – so she needs to monitor his body temperature, show him how she does it and remind him of the connection between clothing and warmth.

Participation is not just about letting children make decisions and leaving them to 'suffer' the consequences – we need to follow through, check the consequences, help children to make any changes necessary.

Judging children's capacity to participate

We have to make judgments about children's capacity to make informed decisions.

For this, we need to consider what we know of the individual child and ask questions like:

- Does he remember past experiences?
- Is he able to look to the future – to imagine, plan and predict?
- Can he put information together – make

associations, understand cause and effect, learn from experience?

A child who can do these things should have the intellectual capacity to participate in decisions that directly affect him.

Where decisions will have a possible impact on others we also need to ask:

- Does he accept responsibility for his actions, or does he protest 'It wasn't me!' when he does something wrong?
- Does he honour agreements made? Can he stick to agreed rules?

Inability to do these things should not prevent children from participating in decisions, but might limit the options we agree to; for example, we are more likely to agree to children moving the contents of the home corner to another part of the room for a picnic if we are confident that they will put them all back when they have finished.

To participate in group decisions, a child needs to be able to:

- listen to other people
- consider points of view other than his own
- co-operate with others.

To participate in any decision, a child needs to be able to:

- know what he wants/what is important for him
- express his feelings
- indicate his preference.

Children who are used to adults doing their thinking for them may find this hard. They will need to start with simple choices between given options and move on, as they gain confidence, to more complex issues.

Desirable outcomes for children's learning

If you are wondering how a participative approach will fit in with the 'Desirable Outcomes' that accompany the nursery education voucher scheme – don't worry. It will help the children to work towards them.

- When they help with cooking, lay tables and rearrange the layout of their room children will be working practically with shape, position, size and quantity. Those who are given a budget and asked to choose equipment will be counting and gaining an understanding of number. All part of the *Mathematics* curriculum.
- Expressing feelings, caring for others and gaining confidence, self-esteem and independence, all contribute to children's *Personal and Social Development*. So do initiating ideas, solving

problems, choosing activities and being able to work in a group.

- *Language and Literacy* will be developed through talking and listening, compiling *All about Me* books, telling and acting stories and responding to those in books.
- The use of art, music and movement as means of expression will contribute to children's *Physical and Creative development* – amongst other things.
- A group of children who design and model their ideal play area will not only be developing *Knowledge and Understanding of the World* but covering all the other areas of the curriculum in one fell swoop!

Preparing for participation

To make it possible for young children to make decisions and take responsibility, the right conditions need to exist. These include:

- *Opportunity*
  Children need the opportunity to try things for themselves. Many parents report that they only discovered how capable their children were when they themselves became incapable, through illness or lack of time, and their children took over tasks the parents would normally have performed.

- *Experience*
  Children who have had the chance to practise skills will become capable of them at an earlier age than those who have not. For instance, children who have been in group care from a young age, or have older siblings, tend to be able to co-operate at an earlier age than those who have not had the experience of mixing with other children.

- *Role models*
  Much of what children learn is gained from watching and listening to other people. As well as learning skills and gaining information from adults, children notice how adults behave; how – for instance – they deal with conflict. What adults *do* has far more impact on children than what adults *say*. Children need the experience of adult role models who 'practise what they preach' – who show children ways of caring, co-operating and

negotiating; who themselves resolve conflict fairly and peacefully; who are prepared to take on challenges, deal with set-backs, admit to mistakes and feel good about their successes.

Beneficial as positive adult role models are, it can be hard for young children to imagine themselves being able to do things that adults do, given the huge differences that they perceive between themselves and adults. Some may believe that it is the very nature of being grown-up that confers ability on adults.

When young children have the opportunity to see older children doing such things as caring for others, standing up to bullying and solving problems they are more likely to believe that these are things that they, too, might be capable of.

So children will benefit both from positive adult role models and from the experience of seeing older children, with whom they can more easily identify, demonstrate capabilities which they can emulate.

- *Expectations*
  As we have seen with the self-fulfilling prophecy, what we expect of children influences both the opportunities we offer them and how children feel about themselves – and thus, how well they achieve. Children who have been told that they are stupid or careless or lazy may begin to believe these things of themselves and either act accordingly or not attempt new challenges for fear of failing.

- *Motivation*
  Children need to know that gaining new skills will open up more possibilities for them and give them more control over their lives. They are more likely to persevere in activities that are enjoyable to them and where their efforts are recognised and encouraged.

- *Information*
  Children need information that is relevant, clear and understandable. As Tizard and Hughes say in *Young Children Learning*: 'the major communication and thinking problems of young children arise, not from inability to reason or compare, but from misinformation, lack of information ...'[15]

At what age can we expect children to ...?

The chart which follows gives a guide to what we can expect of children at different ages.

As with any age-related guide, the capacities relate to developmental norms; that is to say, they are what is expected of the 'average' child – and should, therefore, be treated with caution. Some children will be capable of certain things at a younger age than the norm given and some at a later age. Being two does not necessarily mean you are egocentric and unable to co-operate, just as being 18 does not necessarily mean you are responsible, able to budget wisely and take care of your own needs.

Expectations have to be realistic; there are things that children cannot do until they have reached a particular stage in their development. The point at which this happens is not solely determined by chronological age.

0-18 months

Children of this age range will be dependent on adults to ask the 'right' questions, to interpret their responses, and to take these into account in any decisions that affect the child.

Developmental capacity
- have limited mobility and control over their bodies
- experience the world through their senses
- are wholly dependent on others for provision of their basic needs
- use facial expressions, body language and gesture, and pre-linguistic verbalisation to express feelings and needs and to indicate preferences
- have limited memory span
- are largely egocentric – concerned with own needs and operate on an individual basis
- can respond only to things in the immediate present that they can see, touch, hear, taste and smell
- have limited experience and understanding of danger

Can participate in decisions about
- food
- clothing
- who they want to be with and how they are handled
- what they play with

Methods of participation
- accepting or refusing things offered
- indicating what interests them through gazing intently, turning towards or reaching out for objects or people
- indicating how they are feeling through facial expressions, body movements and responses such as tears and laughter
- indicating preferences between given options
  (the child chooses from options selected by the adult, which take into account the safety, health and welfare of the child)
  – reaching out, grasping or pointing
  – nodding or shaking their heads as options are shown to them
  – nodding or shaking their heads in response to questions with yes/no answers such as 'Do you want milk?'

1½–3½ years

Developmental capacity

- have increased mobility and control over their bodies
- still express many feelings and indicate preferences physically, but are also beginning to use language for these purposes
- increased memory span and ways of expressing themselves enable them to consider options beyond the immediate present; eg child indicates he wants to go on an outing by walking to the front door and saying 'coat on'
- are able to wait and defer wishes for short periods of time
- older children within the age range will play/work in pairs or small groups
- beginning to use language to co-operate and negotiate with others – some sharing and turn-taking possible
- will take part in small-group work provided they can participate actively; eg singing, movement

Can participate in decisions about

- food that they eat and how much
- what they wear
- activities they engage in
- who they play/spend time with
- which, if any, early years group they attend and when

Two children started playgroup at two and a half and were happy as long as their mother stayed – which she did. They told her they would stay on their own when they were three – and they did, happily.

Another child started at two and a half, was fine for the first few weeks, then didn't want to go, so stopped. Six months later he told his mum he wanted to go back to playgroup. He settled well.

A child attended three playgroups in a rural area. He was happy at two, but hid on the floor of the car as he approached the other one. His mum asked if he would like to stop going to that one and was able to arrange extra days at the other two.

Not all parents can be so flexible about their children's attendance at a nursery. But if a child is attending solely for his benefit, he should be able to make choices.

Methods of participation

- choosing between given options as before, plus verbal communication, pointing to pictures, using movement
- suggesting additional options, using language, mime, movement
- express feelings, as before plus using language, mime, movement, painting, music

3½–5 years

Developmental capacity
- can empathise with the feelings of others and consider their needs
- use language to express feelings and ideas, to influence the behaviour of others and to explore more abstract ideas
- use their imagination to explore situations and roles beyond their immediate experience – can explore 'What if …?'
- can co-operate with others, share, take turns, and follow rules – especially those mutually agreed in the course of imaginative play
- spend more time in group activities – interaction with others becoming more important than interaction with objects
- talk about past experience and can look to the future
- have a growing understanding of cause and effect and can begin to consider the effects of their actions on themselves, on others and on their surroundings
- use logic and reason to explain and make sense of the world
- are physically adept at most self-help skills such as dressing, pouring drinks, toileting

Can participate in decisions about
- food, clothes, activities, people, group they attend – as before
- their immediate environment
- buying new equipment
- menus
- routines of the day
- solving problems and conflict resolution
- caring for themselves and others
- rules and boundaries

Methods of participation
As before
- choosing between given options
- suggesting additional options
- expressing feelings and preferences

plus
- compiling scrapbooks/books about themselves
- making representational drawings and models
- discussing issues raised in books
- making up and acting out stories personally or using puppets
- taking part in group activities and discussions in a forum such as Circle Time

6–7 years

Developmental capacity
- can think in more abstract terms
- can consider several aspects of a situation at a time
- can organise own thoughts and plan and carry out schemes individually and in groups
- can problem-solve in groups
- have growing understanding of number, size, space and time
- are able to work with written symbols – words and numerals
- have clear ideas of what is fair and react strongly to injustice
- increasingly aware of 'world' issues, eg poverty, drought, cruelty to animals and environmental damage, and want to do something about them

Can participate in decisions about
As before, plus
- how they will spend their time
- what they learn and how (National Curriculum makes this difficult, but not impossible)
- setting and maintaining rules
- the wider environment, eg housing, play areas
- buying equipment – considering factors such as cost, space, quantity, durability planning menus
- their health needs, medical treatment
- who they live with and where

Methods of participation
As before, plus
- group discussions, brainstorms, examining pros and cons, prioritising
- drama, music and movement
- writing stories, letters, plans
- making maps, posters, books, models
- using cameras and cassette recorders
- attending/speaking at meetings, workshops, demonstrations

A policy for participation

A policy is a statement of intent:
■ this is what we want to happen
■ this is the course of action we shall take to make it happen.

A policy is useful in many ways:
■ It sets out clearly your aims and objectives – the goals you intend to achieve.
■ It informs new workers, parents, students and volunteers what your group believes in and how it operates.
■ It keeps your group 'on target' and makes sure that good intentions do not get lost under the pressure of everyday work.
■ It is a general framework to refer to when you meet new situations and are not sure how to proceed.
■ It can be used as back-up when your way of working is being challenged. (One of the great benefits of the Children Act is that early years groups must now have an Equal Opportunities Policy and this policy can be used to support and validate ways of working previously challenged by some as unnecessary or contentious.)

Drawing up a policy

The process of drawing up a policy for participation will give all adults in your group a chance to discuss what they mean by participation and to agree on practical steps they can take to make it a reality for children.

A suggested approach

1 Involve as many people in your group as possible – those working directly with children, administrative staff, cooks, cleaners, committee members and parents.

2 'Brainstorm' what children's participation means to each of you – in general terms. Write these ideas up. For example:
   ... *children being involved in decisions that affect them*
   ... *children being asked what they think*
   ... *children choosing what they do, eat, wear ...*

3 Discuss your ideas and feelings. Allow plenty of time for this. Bear in mind that adults who have little chance to participate in decision-making processes themselves may wonder why children should have a right to do so.

4 Find one statement about children's participation that you can all agree on.

5 Adopt this as your group's *aim* for participation – what you want to work towards. 'We aim to ...'
   This aim – reached by consensus – may not be for as high a level of participation as some group members would like. What is important is that all group members agree to adopt this aim and to work towards it. A higher level of participation can be agreed at a later stage, after this first attempt has proved successful.

6 Discuss practical ways in which you can work towards your aim. These will be your *goals*.
   Your aim was a general statement of intent and may well have been vague in its wording. Your goals need to be specific and worded in such a way that you will be able to tell whether or not you have achieved them. They do not need to describe in detail how you will achieve them; that comes later.

7 List the goals you all agree on and write them into your policy. Show any members of your group who have not been able to join in these discussions a draft of your proposed policy and ask for their comments.

Remember that many decisions – including, most likely, those you are now making – are made in workers' and committee meetings, in other words, formal meetings of adults. One part of your policy should be that:
■ before you make decisions in adults' meetings, you always consider the impact on children in your group;
■ you will always consider whether it would be possible and appropriate to inform or consult children about any proposals, and how to do this;
■ you make sure that your procedures and timescale allow for this to happen;
■ you consider the children's response to any consultation and take this into account before a final decision is taken.

Setting achievable goals

It might help to look at one aspect of your group at a time, such as: communication, routines and activities, rules. See **Section 2 How are children participating now?** (page 30 below). Your goals could be:
■ The children will decide how some of our equipment budget will be spent.

- We will ask children what rules they want in the group.
- Children will choose what they eat, and how much, of the food offered.
- We will ask children what they think of any changes we are thinking of making in the group before we put them into practice – and we will take what they say into account.

A useful way of recognising a workable goal is the acronym SOAP IT:

- *Specific* not general or vague
- *Observable* to you and to others
- *Achievable* you and the children can realistically succeed in this
- *Performance-directed* achieving an end, not just trying
- *Involving* you and the children really want to do it
- *Time bound* you say when, or by when, it will happen.[16]

Implementing your policy

Take each of your goals and discuss how you will put it into practice. Consider what you may need in terms of:

- *Equipment*
  If children are to serve themselves at lunchtime you may need to buy small serving bowls and spoons.

- *Skills*
  Some workers find it easier to facilitate discussion groups than others; some may need further training in listening skills or helping children to resolve conflict.

- *Time*
  How much of this do you have, and how much will you need for preparation, training, meetings …?

- *Finance*
  How much money will you need for equipment, training, alterations to your premises? Where will it come from?

- *Information*
  What will you need to tell children, parents, students and volunteers?

Making a plan of action

- Prioritise your goals.
- List those you can start to implement immediately and those which require further preparation, resources, and so on.
- Set a timescale for change.

Don't try to take on too much at once – remember the *achievable* part of SOAP IT! Both you and the children will need time to get used to change and to become confident with new ways of working before you move on to the next change.

Choose as your first goal to implement one that:

- the children will notice and benefit from immediately
- will be easy for them to understand and undertake
- will be easy for you to explain
- will require skills and resources that you already have or are easy to obtain
- will be understandable and acceptable to the children's parents.

Set a date by which you will have implemented your agreed goals – your *evaluation* date.

Make sure everyone knows what they will be doing and that they have all they need to do it.

Monitoring your policy

- Carry out observations to see how children are adapting to the new way of doing things. Look to see if all children are taking part – or just those who are older, more confident, or able to express themselves easily. Will younger children 'grow into' the new way of working or do you need to make special arrangements or adaptations for them?
- Listen to children's comments on the new way of doing things.
- Make time at staff/committee/parents' meetings to discuss how the changes are working. Note successes, difficulties and any adjustments that need to be made.

Evaluating your policy

When the date you have agreed for evaluation arrives, ask yourselves:

- Which of our goals have we achieved?
- Which have we not achieved? Why is this – unrealistic goals, insufficient time, lack of commitment?
- What changes have we seen in individual children? individual workers? the group as a whole?

- What feedback have we had from parents?
- What worked most successfully?
- What was most difficult?
- Is there anything we will do differently in the future?
- Are we happy with our *Policy for Participation* or do we need to revise or expand it?
- What will we do next?

Involve the children in evaluating their group and the changes that have occurred by asking what they like and don't like and by using techniques described in Section 3 such as *All About Me* (see page 55), and those for Evaluating the group (see page 68).

Action points checklist

To summarise the issues in Section 1, if you are going to promote participation you will need to have considered:

- *Attitudes*

  about the right of children to participate – your own and those of others involved in your setting

- *Expectations*

  of children's capacity to participate

- *Information*

  what you will need to provide for children, staff members and parents

- *Access*

  physical access, children's mobility, and appropriate methods of participation

- *Budget*

  for extra materials that may be needed, staff training, producing information for parents

- *Time*

  for discussion, preparing materials and information, and programming participatory methods into your curriculum and into meetings and decision-making forums

- *Policies*

  producing and adopting a statement about your group's policy on children's right to participate and how you will implement this.

section 2 How are children participating now?

■ *Communication*

In what ways do children express their feelings and opinions? Who does most of the talking – children or adults? Do you have a regular forum in which the children can talk about things that are important to them?

■ *Rules*

Who makes the rules? Do all the children know them? How do they learn them? What are they for? Who enforces them? Are there the same rules for adults and for children? Can children challenge existing rules or suggest new ones?

■ *Conflict*

How is conflict resolved? What part do children play in resolving conflict?

■ *Caring and co-operation*

If children are upset or hurt, who comforts them – other children, adults, both? When new children start, who shows them around and looks after them while they settle in? Do children help each other with activities and personal needs such as feeding and dressing?

■ *People*

Can children choose which adults and children they spend time with – most of the time, some of the time? If they are divided into groups, can they choose which group they will be in?

■ *Environment*

Can children help to decide how the rooms are arranged? Who decides whether they will play inside or outside? Do they have easy access to all that they need?

■ *Routines and activities*

Who decides how the day or session will be structured? Do the children have any choice about whether and when they sleep and eat? Are they able to decide which activities they take part in, and for how long? Are they involved in planning activities? Who decides where you will go on outings?

■ *Equipment*

Who decides what new equipment will be bought? Can children decide which equipment they would like to have out?

■ *Food*

Are children involved in choosing menus, shopping, preparing, cooking or serving food?

■ *Clothes*

How much choice do children have over what they wear?

■ *Evaluation*

Do you know what children think of the group? How do you find out? Do children have the opportunity to reflect on what they do in the group?

Talking and listening

Young children may not know as much about the world as most adults do but they do know about themselves – how they feel, what is important to them, how they work things out and make sense of the world.

Tape yourself talking with children and compare this with how you talk with adults. Is there a difference in your tone of voice? Are there things you say to children that you wouldn't say to adults?

Consider the list of phrases below. How many of them have you heard said to children? How many have you heard said to adults?

you're not big enough

say please

how old are you now?

say thank you

you're so cute

you must share it

blow your nose

talk properly

you're dribbling

sit still

play nicely

stop fidgeting

say sorry

don't answer back

because I said so

don't be cheeky

you can't have your pudding until you've finished your dinner

If we do not use these words when speaking to adults, is it because:
- *it's not necessary (it is assumed that all adults know how to behave)*
- *it would be rude and insulting*
- *they would be angry?*
What effect do such words have on children?

Children need to be listened to with respect and to have their feelings acknowledged, their perceptions recognised and their ideas welcomed.

In practical terms this means:

■ *Give children the opportunity to talk*

In some settings the adults are so busy doing things that children have limited opportunity to talk to them. The ethos of the group may even be such that an adult who does spend time listening to children will be considered as not really working. Listening to children is important and needs to be recognised and valued as such; time needs to be allocated for it.

As well as providing opportunities for spontaneous conversation, we need to offer a forum in which all children can talk to and listen to each other. Circle Time is one such forum and can be used to discuss issues and exchange ideas, as described in more detail in Section 3.

■ *Be close enough to hear what children say*

We need to be on the same level as children, sitting on small chairs or on the floor or sharing adult-sized chairs with them.

■ *Give full attention to what children are saying*

Focus on the child who is talking and make eye contact. Listen carefully, both to what they are saying and to what they mean to say. If what they are saying does not make sense to you, try and put yourself in the child's place and imagine what he might have been told or seen.

One child told his teacher: 'My dad comes to pick me up from school so I don't get dead'.

He had been told he couldn't walk home from school by himself because a car might hit him when he was crossing the road. Children often say what the consequences of something will be in this way rather than why something is so.

Another example of this is: 'The ground's wet, that why it's raining'.

■ *Don't interrupt children*

All too often we think we know what children are going to say and finish their sentence for them. Sometimes we get it wrong, but not all children are confident enough to tell us – they may just give up trying to communicate with us.
Some children, it is true, have difficulty expressing themselves and need adults or other children to supply them with a word, make connections. They, particularly, need the chance to talk. Many adults will interrupt when children are speaking in a way that would be considered rude if two adults were talking. Interrupting gives the message that what children say is not very important.

■ *Talk respectfully to children*

Children know when they are being patronised – and don't like it any more than adults do. If your standard response is invariably something like 'Oh that's lovely' they will believe either that you are not listening properly or that there is something wrong with your judgment. Children have some sense of the value of what they say and do and need to be helped to develop that by encouraging them to reflect on and evaluate their own efforts.

■ *Be honest with children*

If you don't know something, say so. If you have made a mistake, apologise.

■ *Acknowledge children's feelings*

Telling children that there is nothing to be frightened of is not going to make their fears go away. Think of some of your own irrational fears – spiders, mice, whatever makes you tremble. No one can argue you out of those.

You can acknowledge children's anxieties without reinforcing them by using techniques such as **reflective listening**, echoing to the child either the words she has spoken or the feeling behind the words.

Rather than saying to a child who is crying for her mum: 'It's all right, your mum will be back soon', you could say: 'Yes, you want your mum and you're feeling sad'. You can go on to talk about her mum coming back and try to interest her in other things, but only when she feels she can trust you to know how she is feeling, and that how she is feeling is all right, will she be able to trust anything else that you say or do. Giving voice to feelings can help children to accept and come to terms with them.

■ *Acknowledge children's perceptions*

Children may say things that you know not to be wholly true but which their experience so far tells them are true. A child who insists that dads can't cook is not wrong – he just may not have met one who can. His experience needs to be acknowledged – and then broadened.

■ *Resist the temptation to find the 'teaching point' in every exchange*

Aware of our role as educators, we can feel impelled to impart or test knowledge at every opportunity; for instance:

Child: 'My mum's car broke down on the way to nursery!'

Adult: 'Did it? And what colour is your mum's car?'

There are times when this is appropriate and times when it is not – when it has nothing to do with what the child is telling you, interrupts her flow and moves into your agenda rather than hers.

Exploring children's perception of the rules

If you just ask children to tell you what the rules in your setting are you may run into certain difficulties:

■ *You will be asking them a question to which they know you already have the answer.*

This sets up an unnatural form of communication in which they may feel:
– they are being tested
– it is a trick question
– they are being asked as a prelude to being told off for breaking one of the rules.

■ *Young children may not distinguish between home and group rules/codes of conduct.*

They may be confused by the difference between:
– home rules which may or may not apply in your group
– and group rules which always apply.

■ *Because they live very much in the present young children are likely to tell you of the rules they have been most recently asked to follow.*

If you were to ask them at snack time they might say: 'You can't leave the table if you're still eating'.

To avoid the first of these difficulties, you could ask the children to tell a visiting adult or a new child the rules. For instance:

'At this nursery, we have to …'

'At this nursery, we mustn't …'

'At this nursery, we get told off if we …'

Section 3 contains three more techniques for exploring children's perceptions and understanding of the rules: 'The Naughty Puppet' (see page 63), 'The Fishing Game' (see page 64) and 'A Card Game' (see page 64).

Conflict

Two children are wrestling for possession of the favourite dressing-up shoes. 'I had them first!' cries Laura. 'But I want them!' says Chloe.

Both are getting heated, and there is a strong possibility that someone will get hurt.

What do you do?

Approaches to conflict

We tend to view conflict as something negative: people get hurt, things get damaged, and conflict disrupts the smooth running of the group. We feel that we must deal with it as quickly as possible and get on with more 'important' things. In practice, this often means adults 'sorting things out'.

But how often do we find ourselves returning to the same argument we thought we had resolved five minutes previously? We may have removed the object that was being fought over or imposed some other resolution of our own, but we find that we have not removed the feelings of conflict – nor have we helped the children find their own ways of resolving conflict peacefully and fairly.

Conflict is disruptive, but it does not have to be negative. Where there is injustice, we must struggle against it. Conflict can be a positive force for change. It can also help us develop our strengths, know our own minds, even – if we are prepared to listen – get to know the minds of others.

There will be times when you see children arguing or fighting when you have to intervene immediately – when a child is in physical danger, or when her attempts to handle taunts or abuse from other children are not working.

Other times you may be able to stand back and observe for a few moments what is happening: what the argument is about; what strategies the children are using; who is allying themselves with whom. If the children cannot resolve the conflict themselves and you do have to intervene this observation will give you a fuller picture of what has happened and may suggest ways of approaching the problem.

Mediation

When you intervene, the following process can help the children to resolve their own conflict:

■ *Ask each child to say, or to show, what happened.*

By doing this each child expresses her point of view and hears the other child's point of view (children will need to know, through past experience, or your stating it, that they will not get into trouble by telling you what they did).

■ *Ask each child to say how they feel.*

■ *Acknowledge what is important to each child.*

You can do this by reflecting back some of what they said, for example 'You are angry because Chloe took the shoe you had first'.

■ *Invite suggestions from the children about what they could do now.*

■ *Ask them to choose a solution which everybody will be happy with.*

In the example above, Laura's solution was that Chloe could have the shoes when she had finished with them. Chloe was dubious about this, but brightened when, just a minute later, Laura brought her the shoes.

Conflict between children and adults

In these situations we need to stand back and see things from the children's point of view. It might help if we can imagine a situation in which we might feel as angry, frustrated or unyielding as the child is and so be able to accept the strength of the child's feelings and think of ways of moving forward.

Both child and adult may need a 'cooling-off' period before they come together again to explore ways of resolving the conflict, make their apologies, explain their actions.

When we are angry, we cannot play the mediating role, and may need another adult, or child, to play this for us. We can use situations like this positively to show children how adults cope with conflict, and how both children and adults can help each other to sort things out.

Sharing

Most conflicts between young children are about the possession of objects. 'It's good to share', we tell children, often expecting more of them than we willingly do ourselves. How many of us are happy to lend people money, hand over a book we are halfway through reading, or share our partner with someone else?

To share something, you first need to feel you fully possess it. You also need to have the experience of lent things being returned. As Jennie Laishley points out in *Working With Young Children* we use 'sharing' for three quite different processes:

■ *lending* when a child at home lets a visiting child play with his toys

■ *taking turns* in group care where turns are taken with toys which belong to the group

■ *giving away* when a child 'shares' her sweets.[17]

By insisting that children share, we often undermine the voluntary sharing that children are capable of – like the three-year-old who, noticing that there were three sandwiches left on the plate and more children still at the table, broke each sandwich in half.

Children find turn-taking much easier if they have some control over the process. For instance, 'Can you let him have it when you have finished with it?' may be more acceptable than 'Can you share it?'

'You can't play'

If the argument is about who can join in a game, the same mediation approach can be used, but other issues might need to be considered too.

No child should be excluded from a game for discriminatory reasons such as gender or colour.

If this does happen, you will need to discuss with the children how hurtful and unfair this is and that it is against the rules of your group. You may need to correct wrong information. Plan more activities that challenge bias; work further with parents for their full involvement in your equal opportunities policy and practice.

If it does not involve discrimination, but is about children exercising their choice over who they will work or play with, adult injunctions to allow a child into the game may be neither appropriate nor successful.

For instance, you might get a group of children who are playing in the home corner to accept another player into the game reluctantly – only to find the child has been assigned the role of dad and sent off to work.

As adults, there are people we enjoy spending time with, can exchange ideas and work successfully with, and there are people who irritate us and won't listen, or try to control us. We need to be able to get on with them in a general way, but they are not people we would choose to undertake a project with, or spend time socially with. We have the right to choose our friends, and so do children.

You can't say you can't play

One nursery teacher who no longer believes that children have the right to exclude others from their play is Vivian Gussin Paley. Following a personal experience of feeling lonely and excluded, and recognising that no one can learn and thrive when they feel like this, she decided she wanted a new rule in her kindergarten class: You can't say you can't play.

Following her usual practice, she went about this in a participative way. She introduced the idea to her class:

'Should one child be allowed to keep another child from joining a group? A good rule might be

'You can't say you can't play'.

Out of a class of 25 children four found the idea appealing – those most often rejected. Others reacted with dismay:

'But then what's the whole point of playing?'

She discussed her plan with each of the older classes in the school. Most echoed the younger children's responses:

'Yeah, it's very fair, but I don't think it can work.'

They did add that if she was going to try it, it had to be with the youngest ones:

'(In kindergarten) … they're nice enough to follow a new rule. They trust you.'

'If you want a rule like that to work, start at a very early age.'

Alongside these discussions, Vivian was writing a story, which she told to the children as each chapter was finished. It explored friendship, jealousy and how it feels to be excluded. It was set in the Kingdom of Tall Pines and contained princesses, castles, tiny people and dragons – all the ingredients of a good fairy story – and a wise and magical magpie.

At one point in the story a new boy comes to the Kingdom's school. He appears wild and awkward and the school children won't accept him. His name is Raymond. Vivian's children are troubled by the way he is treated.

'Does Schoolmistress have the rule?' one asks.

'No fair about Raymond,' says another, some chapters later.

'Those kids weren't nice.'

Vivian realises that she has moved the story on without resolving Raymond's problems to her children's satisfaction. She goes back to that chapter and reworks it, incorporating the You can't say you can't play rule. The kindergarten children are pleased.

After weeks of preparing the children, Vivian posted the new rule on their classroom wall and pointed to each word as she read it aloud. The children were uneasy – it seemed too abrupt an announcement. But at the end of the first week of the new rule there had been few mishaps and all were quickly resolved. Some children were still excluding others, but when they did a child would say 'You forgot the rule,' or a teacher would be brought over to say it.

Older children in the school asked how the rule was working. Told that the children seemed to be taking it for granted already one nodded, smiled and said:

'I knew they would. When I was in kindergarten I would have loved that rule. To tell you the truth, I could use it right now.'[18]

Caring and co-operation

A nursery teacher is counting round a circle of three and four year olds to determine the five who will be the first to hunt for hidden Easter eggs. Mollie bursts into tears.

'Mollie, what's wrong? You'll have your turn. We're going round the circle the way we always do'.

Mollie's crying becomes more intense.

'Just go the other way, teacher. Then she'll be first'.

Eric, who usually allows no one to gain an advantage, offers a plan that would place him in the last group to hunt for eggs.

'Then you'll be last.'

'I don't care. Do it! Do it!'

Everyone nods in agreement.[19]

A nursery worker is feeling sad. Throughout the day a four year old child stays by her side. From time to time she pats the worker or slips an arm around her. She says very little, stays close, shows she has noticed and cares.

These young children are able to empathise with others and to consider their needs. They are not egocentric, unable to see things from any viewpoint other than their own. Nor are they unusual.

When children have observed others caring for and co-operating with each other, when they have benefited from this themselves, when they are given the opportunity and encouragement to do so they will help each other out, comfort those who are upset, make personal sacrifices for the benefit of others. Through such actions they will often feel a sense of personal empowerment.

A child involved in a health project aimed at stopping adults smoking said:

'Doing this project has made me feel important, whereas before I thought I was just a kid and couldn't really do anything to help'.[20]

There are many ways in which we can encourage children to help each other:

- checking out children who are hurt or upset;
- making suggestions about what will make another child feel better;
- standing up to bullying;
- helping each other with practical tasks such as going to the toilet, dressing, feeding, carrying equipment.

We need to look for these opportunities and build on them; and we need to recognise and comment positively whenever we see children co-operating and caring for each other.

Environment

The more that children can do for themselves, the more capable and powerful they feel and the less they have to depend on adults for help.

Participation is not limited to children saying what they would like to happen, it is also about enabling them to decide for themselves, wherever possible, what they would like to happen and then being able to make it happen.

Access

Our built environment is on an adult scale, which means that many things will be out of reach of small children. In purpose-built nurseries where architects have been made aware of the needs of young children this may be less of a problem, but for anyone working in premises also used by adults, access can prove to be a major barrier to children's participation.

A child's eye view

Try giving yourself a child's eye view:

- Squat or kneel so that you are at the same height as the children in your group.
- Move around the room.
- What do you see from this height?
- Can you see out of the windows, see pictures on display boards?
- Can you reach door handles, coat pegs, sink taps?
- Would you be able to take yourself to the toilet, get yourself a drink of water?

Find out what the children think:

- Give the children a camera and ask them to take pictures of your setting, both inside and outside.
- Ask them to take pictures of the things they like and those that they don't.

The following story illustrates the use of some of these techniques.

Consulting children on the refurbishment of their housing estate

Refurbishment was taking place on the Patio Estate in South Yorkshire. Adults living on the estate had been consulted about the proposed changes – the children had not.

The estate had a Family Centre run by The Children's Society. The staff were concerned about the way in which these changes were already affecting the children, and began a consultation exercise with three to eight year olds on the estate.

They started by asking the children for their opinions. This did not work – the children didn't understand the questions.

They looked for alternatives. Three children were given a camera and some film. The project leader was a newcomer to the estate, so they were asked to show him around, and to take pictures of things that were important to them. Other children joined them and their child's eye view tour included the 'beach' (a pile of sand where, if they peed on it first, they could make sandcastles), a place where 'big 'uns' took drugs, and a dirty stream where they had made their own bridge with the dismantled wreckage of the bridge the council had built – in what the children considered was the wrong place.

During the summer, seven and eight year olds used a tape recorder to interview each other and younger children. They produced drawings, maps and reports.

Priorities began to emerge.

The children complained of mounting rubbish, empty buildings and damp housing. They wanted their stream cleaned up so they could have frogs and fish in it and wild flowers on the bank.

Most significantly, they wanted a play park in the middle of the estate – not on the other side of the perimeter road where the planners were intending to build one. They said it would be dangerous to cross this road and play in an area where there might be strangers.

A handbook of the children's photographs, drawings and comments – complete with spelling mistakes – was published.

Six of the children, by that time aged five to nine, presented their concerns to decision-makers from the local council. The children opted for a 'proper' meeting on adults' terms sitting at desks, rather than on kids' terms sitting in a circle on the floor.

The council officers promised to feed their concerns into practical proposals.

The play park is now planned for inside the estate and the children are to be involved in designing it.

The project leader says this project has challenged much of his previous experience as a playworker:

'I, like many adults, worked from the premise that I knew best. If there is one point that I'd like to put across to people, it is audit your practice. Ask

children what they think about it and let them guide and steer some of that practice'.[21]

Making changes to the environment

When you know what they think, look at your setting again from the child's eye view:

- Ask the children if there is anything they would like to change and discuss the possibilities.
- Encourage them to draw, paint or model the sort of nursery they would build if they could.
- Even if they are too young to produce recognisable pictures or models, you can still ask them to do this and listen to what they say as they produce their ideas.
- Play a 'let's pretend we are moving house – or nursery – game' and ask the children what they would want to take and where they would put it, or let them show you by doing it.

Try out any of the children's suggestions that are feasible and about which there is general agreement.

Monitor these changes with the children. Some things may not work as intended and it is interesting to discuss why this is, what other factors need to be taken into account, what further changes – or returns to what was before – are necessary.

Finding things

Do all the children know where things can be found? You could check this by playing an *Objects guessing game* during Circle Time.

- Make a collection of items that can be found in your group, eg a pair of scissors, a magnet, a building brick and so on.
- Place them in a bag.
- Bring them out, one at a time, and ask the children to tell you or show you where they belong.

Children cannot take responsibility and make decisions unless they are able to find things for themselves.

It is – arguably – possible for one person to remember where they last put something and be able to find it the next time they want it.

As soon as more than one person is involved there is need for a system – 'a place for everything and everything in its place'. More than that, the system needs to be known to all and usable by everyone in the group.

Labelling

Clear labelling of storage systems helps both children and adults to know where to find things and where to return them to.

This can be done in a number of ways:

- sticking a photo or catalogue picture of the contents on the front of each container, as well as using a written description;
- fixing one piece of the set contained on the front of the container – one brick from a construction set, one pencil, one farm animal;
- where equipment such as musical instruments or woodwork tools are hung on pegboard or permanently displayed on surfaces you could draw round each item so that the children will have a template to match it to when they return it to its place.

Room arrangement

One model for organising space is to divide your room or rooms into 'workshop' areas.

This means grouping related equipment into areas defined by screens, storage units, carpets, chairs or whatever is at your disposal and enabling children to choose, from the equipment available, what they will use.

- A child wishing to make a birthday card for her mother can find, in one designated area, card and paper, pens and crayons, scissors, glue, collage materials, sticky tape – all the things she might need – and a surface on which to work.
- Wooden blocks and construction sets of all types could form another workshop area – arranged around a carpet on which the children can build. Materials for miniature play, such as people, cars and animals could be placed close by.
- Another area could be furnished with equipment for imaginative play – with dressing up materials, home corner equipment, dolls, and equipment for playing hospitals, shops, hairdressers.

These areas remain the same each day, so children can go straight to what they want.

The children have permanent access to all the equipment available to the group. There is no adult deciding that the train set will be out today, the cars and garage tomorrow, and the farm set the next day.

For this system to work, children have to put things away once they have finished using them. This may take some initial encouragement on the part of adults, but those using this system say this presents no particular problems.

The 'workshop' model is more difficult to use if you are operating in a very small space, or if you are using shared space and have to get out and put away every piece of equipment and furniture at each end of the session.

In these situations, you may have to offer the children a limited selection of equipment to use at each session and for the children to be able to ask for particular items that they need.

Some groups have found, however, that children who have few toys at home find a wide choice of equipment in the group confusing – they race from one activity to another and settle at none. These children benefit from being offered a more limited choice of equipment at any one time.

Daily routines and choice of activities

- *Who decides how the day or session will be structured?*
  eg free choice periods, set activities, stories, singing, Circle Time, indoor and outdoor play, snack or meal times, rest periods.
- *Do you offer drinks and snacks at set times?*
  What happens if a child is thirsty or hungry at other times?
- *Do you have a set rest time for all children?*
  What happens if a child doesn't want to rest at these times?
  What happens if a child is tired at other times?
- *Are there any routines that some or all of the children resist?*
  'Children like a routine'. Most of us have said this and it is true – as long as it is a routine that they feel happy with. Many children form their own routines; going to the same activity or adult at the beginning of each session; starting with an energetic activity and then moving to a quieter one, or the other way around; deciding that it must be snack time and beginning to clear the tables so that food and drinks can be set out.

What we have to aim for is a routine that acts as a framework for our activities, rather than a straitjacket; a routine flexible enough to accommodate the differing needs of those in the group and which children can help to change if they wish.

We need to be sensitive to the needs expressed by children – none of us work well when we are hungry, thirsty or tired. We need to allow ample time for children to explore ideas, interests and activities at their own pace. This process cannot happen if their day is divided into adult-determined time slots where children are moved from one set activity to another every 15 to 20 minutes.

Routines that enable children to make choices

Some routines make it possible for children to make choices. Here are some examples.

A 'milk bar' system for snack times

This is how some groups operate.

Cartons of milk or alternative drinks are set out on a table and each has a label with a child's name or identifying picture attached. As children are thirsty they help themselves to their drink. They are encouraged to keep their drink in the drinks area and to clean up any spills – the aim being to increase children's choices, not to expand the adult work load!

If funds allow, fruit, vegetables or bread can be cut into small slices and made available for children who are hungry.

In many groups, coming together for snacks and meals is an important and sociable part of the day. In these groups, a jug of water and cups and healthy 'finger food' could be available throughout each session for children who are thirsty or hungry between meals.

At Wood End Family Project in Coventry, crèche staff set up a drinks and fruit bar, available at all times, so that children could decide for themselves when to have a drink and something to eat. There were 20 children in the group, aged 0-4 years.

At first the children kept asking if they could have fruit and water rather than helping themselves, but they soon realised that it was there for them to have when they wanted it. Initially the children kept spilling water, but as they got used to pouring they became proficient and less was spilt. The children helped staff to wipe up spillages where they occurred. The children told the staff that they really enjoyed eating the fruit.

Staff comment that the activity went very well and feel that in time the children will get used to this as a regular part of the session.

Alternative ways of resting

If you have a set rest time, it will probably follow the midday meal. This is a traditional time for young children to take a nap, partly because there will be fewer staff on duty while some take lunch breaks, and it is easier for those remaining to look after sleeping than active children.

Some children may resist sleep. Some may not be tired; some may regard going to bed as something they do at home, not at nursery; some may view going to bed as something they don't do willingly anywhere!

Rather than trying to insist that all children sleep whether they want to or not, are there other options for those who don't want to sleep?

- Can they take part in quiet activities that won't disturb those sleeping – such as drawing, doing puzzles, looking at books, or listening to stories, perhaps through headphones?
- Can they spend rest time with an older group of children within your setting who do not sleep? There may be older children who would welcome the chance to rest and swaps can be arranged.
- For children who are tired at other times of the day, can you set up a resting space in a quiet area of the room, such as the book corner? Some cushions or mats and some covers are all that is needed – somewhere warm and soft and undisturbed where a child can go to lie down.
- If noise from other children cannot be avoided, a taped story listened to through headphones might enable a tired child to switch off from the general buzz and drift into sleep.

Making choices

'Where do you want to go?' 'What would you like to do first?'

In the world of computer software, particularly of the educational variety, children are frequently asked these questions. A range of options is given and the child chooses between them, basing her decision on where she is starting from, what interests her and what she needs to know.

The challenge for all early years workers is to give children the same ability to make decisions and control their own activities in the real world as they are being offered in the 'virtual world' of computers.

We are going to look at:

- the patterns which are revealed when children have a free choice of activity
- how children can participate in constructing their own curriculum within a system of structured adult support and guidance.

Free choice: *Schemas*

Some people believe that children will only learn from formal adult instruction – that they are not capable of following a self-chosen strand of learning in a purposeful way. However, observations of young children's activity within free choice early years settings have shown that there is often a pattern to their activity.

One way in which children have been observed constructing their own curriculum is through following a pattern of action and thought, where they explore one particular concept through many diverse forms. These patterns – known as *schemas* – have been detailed in a number of books and articles, and a brief description is given here.

The names given to observed schemas vary, but some of the most commonly noticed are:

■ *Enclosure or enveloping*
One thing inside another (see below)
■ *Connection*
Exploring ways of joining things, and people, together
■ *Transporting*
Moving self and objects from one place to another
■ *Trajectory*
Exploring paths and lines made by self or objects
■ *Rotation*
Exploring circular movements and shapes
■ *Orientation*
Exploring different viewpoints

So a child whose current schema is 'enclosure' – one thing inside another – might be observed during a session doing all of these activities:

■ enveloped in dressing-up clothes
■ making enclosures with building blocks or dens from furniture covered with blankets
■ enclosing playdough cherries in a playdough pie
■ filling bags with smaller items, wrapping presents and stuffing paper into envelopes
■ representing the enclosure scheme visually through drawing borders around her pictures, covering her paintings with layer upon layer of colour
■ enjoying stories such as 'There Was An Old Woman Who Swallowed A Fly'.

At first glance, such a child may seem to be lacking in concentration, flitting from one activity to another without any apparent connecting thread. But closer observation reveals a discernible pattern to her actions. She is making sense, through every means available to her, of that aspect of the world which is to do with enclosing, enveloping and containing. Through physical action, the arrangement of materials, language and representational means, she is making connections in her own brain that will allow her to fully understand and work with the concept of 'inside'.

Knowing about schemas has helped parents and early years workers to:

■ *See a positive purpose in behaviour that had seemed puzzling or even annoying*
For example, the child who ties table legs up with string may be doing so as part of his 'connection' schema.
■ *Offer acceptable substitutes for unacceptable activities*
So a child dropping toys down the toilet as part of a 'trajectory' schema could be offered marbles and a chute.
■ *Predict what might next interest a child*
Make available materials and experiences that will support and extend her learning.

Most children will explore one schema up to a certain point and then move on to another; some will explore more than one at a time.

For children to develop their understanding of the world through schemas they need:

■ access to a wide range of materials, activities and experiences
■ flexibility to use these in ways that will serve their schema
■ time in which to explore at their own pace
■ adults who recognise the importance of what they are doing and who can observe, support and nourish their schema by offering appropriate materials and experiences and by talking with the children about their activity, offering vocabulary to describe the concepts they are exploring, and suggesting ways in which they could further their experience of these concepts. [22, 23]

Making choices within a system: *High/Scope*

Let us proceed on the basis that children can participate in constructing their own curriculum as long as they are given the right conditions and support.

One approach to the curriculum that offers these, and that is being used successfully in the US and in a growing number of early years settings in this country is *High/Scope*.

Background

High/Scope is an approach to the curriculum that encourages children to make choices and decisions, to solve problems and to reflect on what they have done and learned.

It is based on the following principles:

■ *Certain key experiences are central to young children's development.*

These are grouped under the headings of:
- social relations and initiative
- creative representation
- music and movement
- language and literacy
- classification, seriation, number, space, time.

■ ***Key experiences occur most often when children are actively learning.***

ie when they are handling materials, talking about what is happening, experimenting and exploring for themselves.

■ ***Adults should take an interactive role.***

Observing, supporting and extending the children's interests, knowledge, skills and understanding.

■ ***The environment should be arranged in a logical way***

Children should be able to help themselves to what they need. For examples of this, see the sections on room arrangement and labelling on page 36

■ ***Working in a team, and working with parents, is beneficial.***

'Plan – do – review'

High/Scope follows a routine based on: 'plan – do – review'.

This is an example of how the daily routine operates based on a session lasting two and a half hours.

1 ***Circle time*** (5-10 minutes)

Greetings, 'talk about'/news time, and a chance to discuss rules, expectations or any other group management issues.

2 ***Planning time*** (approximately 15 minutes)

Children split into smaller groups, each with one adult, and plan what they will do during work time. Each child chooses from a range of available options and can be reminded of these options by planning aids. For example:

planning bag – a bag with a selection of materials on offer and/or products previously made with these;

photographs

– of each area of the environment

– of equipment that is in each area

Children might indicate their choice in one of a number of ways:

■ fetch something they want to work with

■ point to an area in which they want to work

■ point to a photo of what they want to work with

■ say what they want to do

■ place their name card or photo by a picture of their chosen activity

■ draw what they want to do

■ dictate or write what they want to do

■ record on a tape recorder what they want to do.

Making a plan is a way of helping children to choose – it is not a binding contract. Their plans might change, and often do.

3 ***Work time*** (1 hour)

Children get the materials they need and work on their plans – or change plans if they wish. They put away materials as they finish with them. The role of the adults is to:

■ observe;

■ support children in their use of materials and attempts to solve problems;

■ participate – giving the message that the children's activity is important, demonstrating techniques, role modelling behaviours;

■ extend the children's thinking and language, as appropriate.

4 ***Tidy-up time*** (10 minutes)

A signal is given that tidy-up time is approaching; this could be a whistle or turning the lights off/on. Children put materials back where they belong, with adult help and encouragement.

5 ***Review time*** (10 minutes)

In the same small groups as for planning, children indicate what they did during work time. They can use the same strategies for doing this as they used at planning time. They may talk about what went well, any problems encountered, any solutions that they found or might try another time. Sometimes they will talk about what they would like to do the following day.

6 ***Snack time*** (5-0 minutes)

Children help themselves to drinks and help others with drinks, as necessary.

7 ***Small group time*** (15-20 minutes)

In small groups, again with one adult, children take part in an activity planned by that adult and based on what he or she has noticed during previous observation. The activity may be designed to meet particular needs of children within the group – to practise a skill, use language, encourage co-operation. Or it may be designed to introduce the children to an activity that none of them has yet chosen during work time.

The small group time ends with a story or music.

As can be seen, the High/Scope approach includes both child-planned and adult-planned activities. This combination enables children to reap the benefits of self-chosen activity – exploring what most interests and is relevant to them at that point, and therefore being well-motivated and likely to persist and concentrate in what they are doing. The adult-planned activity ensures that children don't 'over-specialise' and miss out on activities that may give access to other key experiences they need in order to develop fully.

The example of a daily routine summarised above is just one aspect of the High/Scope approach. [24]

Choosing equipment

- How do you decide what your equipment budget will be spent on ?
- Do the children play any part in this decision?
- Do you think they should?

It is tempting, particularly where budgets are limited, for adults to decide what new equipment should be bought. They base their decision on their knowledge and experience of the appropriateness for the age or stage of the children in the group; challenge offered; suitability for group play; durability and so on. We are afraid that children might be attracted by bright colours, gimmickry or the lure of the latest television craze, and choose toys that will fall apart, be discarded as having limited play value after only a short time, or cause problems of sharing.

In thinking through your approach to the question of whether children should participate in choosing equipment, ask yourself:

- Have I ever bought something that fell apart, didn't do what I thought it would do or was a waste of money?
- Did I learn anything from such mistakes? If so, what?
- What opportunity do young children have for learning lessons such as these?
- What information do they need to help them in their choosing?
- If, having done this, you decide that the children should be involved in the choice of equipment, try the following:

1 *Adults choose and consult with children*

- Decide how much of your budget will be spent on items that you will choose – necessary replacements; filling gaps that you perceive in your provision; basic materials such as paper and paint.
- Decide how you will spend this part of your budget and show the children pictures of what you propose buying.
- Explain why you have chosen this equipment and, if appropriate, how you as a group of adults decided among different options suggested.
- Take note of the children's comments – you may decide to modify your choice in the light of these.
- Let the children know your final decision and how, if at all, it has been influenced by their comments.

2 *Children choose*

- Allocate a proportion of your budget for the children, as a group, to choose how to spend.
- Tell the children that you would like them to choose some new toys for the group.
- Discuss with them the possibility that different children within the group may want different things; that they might choose more things than they have the money for and that they will need to agree a fair way of making their final choice.
- Invite suggestions for what this might be, and offer some of your own, such as:
  – the toys that the biggest number of children choose
  – the toys they can all agree would be good to have
  – some toys for the younger children and some for the older.
- Show the children, in some tangible form, how much money they have to spend. You could use counters, straws, beads and make one of these stand for – say – £10.

  The children may not fully understand this yet, but it might prove helpful later on when matching their choices to the money available. You are also letting them know, at the outset, that there is a limit to how much can be bought.
- Proceed with whatever method you feel appropriate to discover the children's choices.

A case study which describes some methods that were tried to find out what playground equipment children would prefer is given below, and two techniques for choosing equipment can be found on page 61.

Monitoring use of the equipment

Once the equipment has been bought – both your choices and those of the children – observe whether it is used, how and by whom. Evaluate how well it meets its aims and discuss with the children their perceptions of it and yours.

Reflecting on choices made is a valuable experience for all and gives the chance to learn from experience, think about what we might do differently in the future, and acknowledge and feel good about successful choices.

Consulting children on upgrading playgrounds

A case study

A group of playworkers in Swansea were asked to consult with children aged 0-12 about their views on 16 playgrounds which were due to be upgraded. They visited children in local schools and parent and toddler groups, as well as carrying out site visits.

They began by using puppets and parachute games, thinking that these would be both an appropriate and a fun way in which to communicate with young children and to find out what playground equipment they would prefer.

In practice, these methods did not work with the younger children. The puppets proved so popular that the children tended to say 'yes' to every option. The parachute games failed in a similar way. When they were asked to run across the parachute if they liked swings, for instance, younger children would run anyway – because they liked the parachute. Only those of around six years old and over were prepared to follow the rules of the parachute game.

What proved more effective was for the playworkers to cut out pictures of possible equipment from catalogues and ask children to point at the equipment they liked best.

The younger children tended to choose pictures of big coloured slides and theme equipment such as pirate ships. Older children – of eight or nine upwards – preferred modular structures which they said they could imagine to be whatever they pleased. Older brothers and sisters offered guidance about the preferences of their younger siblings. They suggested, for example, that they might enjoy train tracks painted on the ground – so they could chuff around on them.

A summary of the children's preferences was presented to Swansea City Council, which had financed the consultation. The designs that followed were disappointing – they failed to reflect the children's suggestions adequately. The local council, while wanting to fulfil children's aspirations, was restricted by its budget. [25]

What can we learn from this case study?

- ***You have to find an appropriate way of consulting with young children.***
What appeared to be an imaginative and exciting way of consulting with young children – the use of puppets and parachute games – failed in its primary aim which was to elicit children's preferences. It did, however, succeed in engaging the children.

- ***Children have to understand the aim of the exercise.***
Problems arose with this method because the children did not understand the aim of the exercise – to choose equipment for playgrounds. Their own aim was to enjoy both puppets and parachute as fully as possible: agreeing with all that the puppets said and moving across the parachute at every opportunity. If there is something that children enjoy doing, they will do it as often as possible – they will prefer to engage than not to engage.

   The method that proved more effective – choosing from pictures – had an aim that could more clearly be understood by the children. Those familiar with catalogue shopping would have had a context into which they could fit this activity. It was – in a way – more real.

- ***For children to express real preferences, they need experience of the choices on offer.***
The younger children did tend to choose the more 'glossy' packages of equipment; they went for colour and for theme equipment such as the pirate ship. The older children chose more open-ended equipment on which they could use their imagination.

   We could say that the older children realised the limitations of packages of equipment intended for one main purpose. Children need the experience of using both kinds of equipment at different stages of their lives, in order to discover for themselves the potential of each.

- ***Children have to understand what the money can buy.***
Where there are budget constraints, these need to be explained in some way to the children. The danger otherwise is that children's hopes will be raised at the prospect of getting all that they have

chosen, and then dashed when they learn that they won't. If we ask them what they would like and then offer something different they may feel either that they are not being listened to or that their views are not acceptable to us. Neither of these feelings is likely to encourage future participation.

Food

What sort of choices do you offer children regarding food? Can they:

■ decide which of the food offered they will eat
■ decide how much they will eat
■ choose from a set menu
■ participate in planning menus?

Encouraging a positive attitude to food

We want children to have a positive attitude towards food and to eat food that is good for them. We also aim to show them the connections between food and health so that they can choose a healthy diet for themselves.

■ *Respect the right of children to refuse food they dislike.*
No child should be forced to eat food that she does not like. This may seem an obvious point, and none of us would physically force-feed a child, but how often have you heard adults saying 'go on – just try a bit', 'just another spoonful' or 'if you don't eat your dinner you won't have any pudding'. The child may acquiesce in the short term but is unlikely to embrace foods previously forced on her when, at a later stage, she does have a choice. Persistent pressure to eat can develop in a child a whole set of attitudes towards food that have more to do with resistance than enjoyment.

When faced with a child refusing food, it can help to think about foods you don't like. How would you feel if made to eat them? Were there foods you were made to eat as a child that you never touch now? What has persuaded you to try new foods – or to try again foods that you used to dislike?

■ *Let children decide how much they will eat.*
Even when we like a particular food, we can be overwhelmed by too large a plateful. The thought of having to eat it all spoils the pleasure of even the first mouthful.

As soon as children are physically able, they can be given the opportunity to serve themselves with the amount they want. Let them take only a small amount if they wish; they can always come back for more.

When first presented with this choice, some children may take more food than they can eat. You will need to make sure they become aware of this, realise that the uneaten food will be wasted and understand why this is a bad thing. It takes experience to know just how much we are likely to eat – even as adults we find that our eyes can be bigger than our stomachs!

Some children will take and eat more than their fair share. They need to be encouraged to consider the rights of others to share in the food available and to work out ways to make sure everyone gets a fair share.

■ *Let children participate in preparing and cooking food.*
On a practical level, the more that children are involved in making meals, the more likely they are to eat them.

The most adventurous children that I have worked with as far as food is concerned were at a community day nursery where everyone who wanted to took turns to cook. Each day one nursery worker took a small group of children to the local shops and market to buy food for the day. The children became friendly with the traders and often got to taste before they bought. The choice of menus was a joint effort between children and adults, based on the nursery's aim of providing healthy meals, often vegetarian, and using wholefoods, fruit and vegetables, and influenced by the children's preferences.

Shopping done, the group returned to the nursery. A long counter divided the kitchen from the dining room and the children stood – on chairs – at the dining room side of this, the adult at the kitchen side.

The children chopped vegetables and fruit, grated cheese, beat eggs, kneaded bread dough – whatever was required and within their capabilities.

They laid the tables, served themselves from bowls of food set on the tables, and cleared and stacked their plates after eating. Sometimes they would help to wash up.

Through their participation these children:

■ developed a positive attitude to food and a willingness to eat a wide range of food – including brown rice and all sorts of fruit and vegetables;

- learnt about the properties of different foods, how they could be used, and something of their nutritional value;
- learnt how to cook, and that cooking could be enjoyable; (Many years later I learned that the four year old boy who had conquered the art of separating eggs for soufflées had gone on to train as a chef.)
- were passing on what they had learned to their families. Another four year old showed his mum how to make a chocolate and orange cake – remembering both quantities and method exactly;
- felt they were engaging in real and important tasks – the sort of things that grown-ups actually do – and thus developed their own confidence and self-esteem.

It is not just in early years settings that children can participate in these ways – many will be doing so at home. And not all nurseries will be able to involve children so actively in preparing meals, especially where food is cooked in a distant kitchen to which the children cannot have access.

What is important is to provide as many opportunities as possible for children to handle, taste, work with and talk about food.

At Park Children's Centre in Liverpool, lunchtime had been a very routine and not particularly enjoyable part of the day. Food was served onto the plates in the kitchen and some of the children were reluctant to eat.

The workers decided to change the way things were done, so that the children, aged 2-4 years, could serve themselves from bowls on their tables.

They noticed improvements from the very first day.

- *Children enjoyed the opportunity to serve themselves with the amount and type of food they wanted.*
- *Lunchtime became more enjoyable for children and workers, and children ate more in this happier environment. The cooks also preferred the new system.*
- *Children were eating more of what the staff describe as good food.*
- *One child who had never eaten any of the nursery food (he brought sandwiches from home) began occasionally to serve himself with small amounts of food and eat it. He became part of the group at mealtimes.*
- *Staff found that the new system was less work for them – and easier to operate – than the old.*

Interestingly, the first day they tried it was a day when they were short-staffed.

Resource implications

- *The childcare workers needed to work closely with the cooks and keep them up-to-date with the changes, as their routines were affected as well.*
- *The group needed to buy more suitable equipment, such as child-sized dishes.*

Lunchtime has now become one of the nursery activities rather than a routine chore. Each day two children count how many are in the group, set the tables accordingly and put out the right number of towels for hand washing. In this way, they practise mathematical skills as well as helping with the social organisation of the group.

Planning menus

One way of inviting children to participate in menu planning while ensuring a balanced diet is for adults to draw up a range of healthy options and ask children to choose among them.

The healthy options will need to be meals that the children are likely to eat, so you will need to find out what foods the children in your setting like, select those that are healthy, and plan menus using these.

Finding out what foods children like

- Ask them to tell you and/or refer to any information they have already given in their preferences, eg in scrapbooks or *All about me* books (see page 55).
- Cut pictures of food from magazines, or draw pictures, and ask children to point to those they like. Or attach paper clips to each picture and use the 'Fishing Game' technique described on page 64.
- Call out names of food, or show pictures, and ask children to show you whether that food makes them feel happy or sad. You could use happy/sad faces, gesture such as thumbs up/down or other techniques described in this handbook.
- Have tasting sessions of samples of food and note the children's comments.
- Observe which of the foods you already offer children choose to eat.
- Ask children's parents or carers. Some children, however, will refuse food at home that they will eat elsewhere, and vice versa.

Choosing from these options

- Each option is represented visually and each child chooses his favourite. He could indicate this by pointing, 'catching' it (as above), fixing a sticky dot label to it, or whatever method you find works best. (If you find that some children are being unduly influenced by the choices of others in the group, you could ask each child to whisper his favourite option to you.) Every chosen option goes onto the menu, over a period of time.

■ Each option is called out or shown and children indicate whether they like or dislike it – using techniques above. All options that at least some children like will form part of future menus.

The approach just outlined draws on children's expressed preferences and lets them choose from adult-selected healthy options.

What it does not do is give children the information that they will need in order to make healthy choices in other settings or in the future, or to plan menus from scratch.

For this you will need to embark on a wider educational programme, looking at:

■ the connection between food and health/growth

■ what particular foods are good – and bad – for

■ how we plan a balanced and varied diet, eg choosing something from each of the four 'food groups'

■ foods that some people don't eat for religious or cultural reasons, or because they have allergies to them

■ foods that children are not familiar with; for instance, extending the range of options open to them through taste-and-try sessions

■ preparation and cooking times needed for foods, and the time available

■ cost.

Being able to consider all these factors together is too complex for children of the age range we are considering and it would be unrealistic to expect them to be able to plan entire menus.

But when you feel that they have an understanding of some of these factors, you could:

■ look again at their favourite foods and discuss what, in health terms, they are good for and bad for

■ invite their suggestions as to how they can restrict their consumption of foods that are 'naughty but nice'

■ make collages showing foods from each of the four 'food groups' and invite children to use these to plan some meals.

At Fair Isle Nursery in Kirkcaldy, staff took photos of existing snack choices, mounted them on card and laminated them. The cards were put in a box and the children presented their choice to the staff.

There were 10 children aged between 18 months and 4 years.

Staff found that:

■ *noticeably more fruit was being eaten*

■ *one 3 year old took on the role of 'adult' and asked other children to choose what they wanted as a snack. She then told the adult, and served the children with their choice.*

■ *the children co-operated and even the youngest appeared to see the sense in what they were trying to do.*

They add:

'This is going to be part of our normal nursery routine and we would encourage colleagues to do the same. This activity has been successful because of the interest and co-operation of all members of the team, including the cook.'

Getting started

Sharing responsibility with children and finding ways to enable them to participate in decision-making may seem like a totally new way of working, and one which will be dauntingly difficult.

But don't be put off – it need not be!

You will probably be using some of the suggested techniques already – maybe without even realising that they are part of a participatory approach.

Some are very simple to use and fit easily into your normal programme. One project which tried out the Toy Catalogue technique commented:

It didn't really take up much time. We looked upon it like an activity just like we would craft or baking … I wouldn't have believed a child of 2½ could have been able to understand what was being asked of her so easily.

Some changes to a participative routine actually mean less work for staff, as workers at one centre found when they started to let children serve themselves at lunchtime.

A five year old in a project where children had drawn up their own rules was asked what happens when someone breaks the rules. 'We don't', she replied.

You have coped with changes like this before. Think back to when you first started working to an Equal Opportunities policy. There were almost certainly things you weren't sure of.

- How would you talk about race, gender and different ability in terms that the children could understand and relate to?
- What were the 'right' things to say?
- Where would you get materials and ideas for activities from?
- How would you convince dubious colleagues or parents that young children need this information and experience?

You didn't do it all at once and you didn't feel confident all at once. You probably made mistakes – and learnt from them.

- You started from where the children were, building on their lives and experience so far.
- You introduced new activities gradually, drawing on one of your greatest resources – the children's

parents – for ideas, materials and practical help.
- You expanded out from this base and into the wider community when you and the children were ready.
- You became more informed, collecting information from television, books, other workers and parents.
- You went on training courses that increased your awareness and gave you practical ideas.

The same will be true with children's participation.

- Introduce it gradually.
- Proceed at a pace you are comfortable with.
- Use all the resources – human and other – that you can.
- Discuss your fears, share your achievements and admit to your mistakes – the children will respect you even more for this.
- Use what is appropriate to your group and the children and staff you work with – not all the techniques will be right for you.
- Make adaptations if you want to. These are suggestions, not tablets of stone.

Have fun!

Finding out what is important for children

Some children can express themselves easily and willingly, some may need adults – or other children – to interpret their feelings and thoughts and to make associations for them.

There are many ways in which to get to know what is important for each child and some of these methods are described in general terms below:

- ***Observation***

This may be of a systematic kind where you decide to observe closely over a set period of time, or it may be anecdotal where you note significant events and conversations.

Observing fantasy or role play will often allow you to see children operating at their highest level as they negotiate with others, use their imagination and solve problems.

- ***Talking and listening***

This is particularly useful when the child is given

the opportunity to take the lead and initiates conversations. The subject will be relevant and meaningful to her and within the scope of her own experience and understanding.

As soon as children are able to listen to each other, take turns and wait for short periods of time, you might want to introduce some sort of group discussions such as Circle Time.

■ Stories and drama

Through stories children can explore most of the important things in their lives:
- experiences that are familiar or new
- family relationships
- feelings such as fear, jealousy and sadness.

Stories provide experiences at second hand. Through them children can explore their feelings, and issues that are sensitive to them, in a secure and supportive environment. For instance, a child who is finding it difficult to express his feelings about his parents' divorce may be able to talk about what us happening to a character in the book who is going through the same thing; how he feels, what he might do.

Children will often link their own experiences to those they hear about in stories, particularly if there is the opportunity to comment and question while stories are being told or read.

Another use of stories – described by Vivian Gussin Paley in her books – is to encourage individual children to tell their own stories to an adult who writes them down. At some later point in the day the children gather in a group to act out the stories.

The stories may be very short, and prompted by external events:

Batman goes whoosh. In the Batmobile.

They may grow out of something the child has experienced. This is Frederick's story, told over four days:

Monday

Frederick Water.

Tuesday

Frederick Once there was water. You drown yourself. You stay under water.

Wednesday

Frederick Water. Then you drown. Water. And then you drown.

Thursday

Teacher Did a bad thing happen in the lake, Frederick?

Frederick No.
Teacher In a swimming pool?
Frederick Yeah, I drowned.
Teacher Who pulled you out?
Frederick My sister took me out. In South Beach. In a pool. I went under again. And I went under again. Then my sister took me out. [26]

■ Puppets

Some children who find it difficult to tell another person what is happening in their lives may find it easier to talk to a puppet. A puppet will not interrupt, show strong emotional responses, or feel the need to answer back. A child can confide in a puppet and – at one remove – with the person who holds the puppet. That person can make encouraging responses, acknowledging what the child is saying or feeling without becoming directly involved in conversation with the child.

■ Dolls

Children will, spontaneously, act out with dolls many of the experiences that they have been part of or witnessed. You see children in the home corner caring tenderly for their dolls, telling them off, smacking and shaking them.

In imaginative play with miniature dolls, children will sometimes reveal their feelings about their family or friends, as Dibs did by repeatedly burying his (father) doll in the sand pit during play therapy sessions. [27]

Adults can also use puppets and dolls in a planned way with children to act out situations, feelings and responses.

■ Painting and drawing

Children sometimes find it easier to express themselves in visual rather than verbal ways. Their paintings and drawings can show how they feel about themselves and those around them. Some times children express things in this way that they don't consciously know about themselves.

In drawings of people, children can show happiness, sadness or anger through a mouth turned up or down, tears on the face, bared teeth and so on.

How big or small they draw themselves in relation to others may indicate how children are feeling about themselves – as may where they position themselves; for instance, inside or outside the family group.

Children may use colour to express different feelings. One childcare consultant uses the concept of 'hurt' colours to enable children to show her what experiences have made them, or will make them, feel hurt.[28]

Children may paint – and then paint over – people they would like to disappear, like the new baby in their family.

■ *Scrapbooks*

Children can show things and people that are important to them by choosing pictures and pasting them into their own book.

■ *Making models*

Children designing play areas or other physical environments often find it easier if they can make a model of what they would like.

■ *Games*

Games can be devised which will enable children to tell you things, such as:
   – what they think of the activities and rules in your setting
   – who they like to be with

   – which toys and equipment they would like to buy.

■ *Music and movement*

Children can use their bodies to express how they feel and to indicate their preferences.

On the following pages you will find descriptions of specific techniques that can be used to help children to:

- express feelings and preferences
- make choices
- solve problems
- work together as a group.

[Thanks and acknowledgment to Frankie Galloway, whose book *Personal and Social Education in the Primary School* Pergamon Educational Productions, 1989, contains many of the activities suggested here]

Participatory techniques

Aim of technique	Title of technique	Page	Age range	Extra resources *Over and above the basic resources found in most groups, such as art &craft materials, balls/bean bags, toy catalogue*	Ease of use see below
Develop confidence and self-esteem	photo displays		3+	Photos of children	1
	self-portraits		4+		1
	badges		3–5+		1
Develop group co-operation	group mimes		6+		2
	individual mimes		6+		2
	problem mimes		6+		2
	pass the mask		3+		1
	touch a shoe		3+		1
	centre throw		4+		2
	circular chair		4+		2
	farmyard animals		4+	animal pictures	1
	build a machine		5+		2
Facilitate discussion	Circle time		3+		1
	brainstorming		5+		3
Expressing feelings and opinions	All about me books		3+		1
	telling & acting stories		3+		2
	feelings drama		4+		2
	When you ... I felt ...		4+		1
	feelings photos		4+		1
	musical feelings		6+		3
	happy/sad lines		3+		1
	happy/sad mats		3+		1
	happy/sad trains		2+		1
	thumbs up/down		2+		1
	happy/sad masks		3+		1
Making choices	pros and cons		6+		2
	toy catalogue		3+		1
	toy shop		5+		2
Exploring specific issues					
Conflict	using puppets		3+	puppets	2
	using stories		4+		2
Rules	the naughty puppet		2+	puppets	2
	fishing game		3+	magnetic rod	1
	card game		4+		2
People	who we like to be with – 1		2+	camera/photos	1
	who we like to be with – 2		3+	photos & magnetic rod	1
	adult roles		4+	photos, tape recorder & visiting interviewer	2
Environment	designing a play area		3+	camera	3
Evaluation	questionnaire		4–7	'interpreter'	1
	taped interviews		3+	tape recorder & interviewer	1
	good things/bad things		6+		3
	picture game		2–4	camera	2
	beans in a jar		5+	dried beans	2
	me at nursery		2+	1:1 adult attention	1

1 easy to explain, easy for children to do, requires little preparation

2 involves skills some adults may not feel confident about or involves children following a series of instructions

3 more detailed planning & preparations or more complex thinking processes for children

Activities to develop confidence and self-esteem

Photo displays

Resources	a photo of each child in the group display board paper and pens
Age range	3+
Method	• Children mount their photos on display board, leaving some space around each. • Ask each child to say something about themselves – it could be something they are good at, that they are interested in or anything they want to say. • Adult or child writes this on a piece of paper and mounts it next to the child's photo. (This caption could be cut out in the shape of a speech bubble). Add any other positive comments that other children make about each child.

Self-portraits

Resources	large sheets of paper thick pencil or felt pen mirror 'people' paints or crayons – ie full range of skin and hair colours scissors
Age range	4+
Method	1 Child lies on paper and another child or adult draws around them. 2 Children paint or draw their own features, skin, hair and clothes within this outline, checking in mirror if necessary 3 Children cut out their figures – with help if necessary 4 Mount them around the room 5 Captions, as described above, can be added to each portrait. *Note* Younger children find filling in a whole body outline too much. They could be given a circle of paper and draw or paint just their face and hair.

Badges

Resources	These can be made from card with a safety pin attached to the back or on large self adhesive labels
Age range	3+–5+
Method	• *Decorative names* (3+) Children write their name on a badge – or you write for them. They then decorate their name badge as they choose. • *Something I'm good at* (5+) The children write their name on a badge and one thing they feel they are good at. • *Thank you* (5+) Children and adults can give badges to express thanks for help, kindness, etc. Younger children could decorate a badge and add kisses, ticks or other symbols to express thanks. Older children could write a message on the badge. • *Congratulations* You can reward achievement of all types by making a badge that records that achievement and giving it to the child to wear; for example, to a child who manages to wait for his turn or a child who finds a peaceful solution to a conflict.

Activities and games to develop group co-operation

Many traditional games depend on there being winners and losers. The games described below promote physical activity, fun and the feeling of being in a group. They encourage children to work together rather than in competition with each other.

One good source of co-operative games is the book *Winners All*, published by Pax Christi.

Group mimes

Age range   6+

Method
1 Divide the children into small groups, four or five to a group.
2 Give each group a scenario that they will mime – something simple and visual, eg going on a train journey, building a sand castle, having a bath.
3 Allow a few minutes for each group to plan and rehearse what they will do – younger children may need help in thinking of suitable actions.
4 Each group then acts out its mime in turn.
5 The other children guess what the mime was about, and comment on how the idea was conveyed.

Individual mimes

Age range   6+

Method
1 Collect ideas for individual mimes, eg:
- It is your birthday. You have been given a big present. You unwrap it carefully and inside you find a kitten.
- You have gone to a friend's house for dinner. His dad has served you and there is something on your plate that you really don't like, but you don't dare tell him.
2 Give each child one of these ideas.
3 The child acts it out.
4 The others guess what it is about and comment on how the actor portrayed the idea.

Problem mimes

Age range   6+

Method
1 One child is given a problem to mime
eg You've gone to the toilet. The wind blows the bathroom door shut and you can't reach the handle to open it and get out.
2 The other children guess what the mime was about.
3 They all think together about possible solutions to the problem.

Pass the mask

Age range   3+

Method
1 The children sit in a circle.
2 One child is chosen to make a funny face to the child on her or his left.
3 That child makes the same funny face as he or she is shown and then makes one of her or his own to the next child – who repeats it back and then makes one of her or his own to the next one in the circle.
4 Thus each child in the circle has a turn to imitate and invent a funny face.

Touch a shoe

Age range	3+

Method

1 Children sit in a circle.
2 One player calls 'Everyone touch a shoe' (or another object or colour).
3 Players must touch something on a child next to them.
  Endless variations of what to touch are possible, eg touch a left ear with a right thumb.
4 This game can be played in slow motion – some children enjoy moving ver-r-ry slowly!

Centre throw

Resources	a ball or a bean bag
Age range	4+

Method

1 Children form a circle with one player standing in the centre.
2 The centre player throws the ball to any child in the circle and runs immediately to any other player.
3 That player runs to the centre of the circle to catch the ball thrown by the last player receiving it.
4 The game continues until all have been the centre player.

This will only work as a smooth flowing game with children who can throw and catch with accuracy. Where younger children wanted to join in, one group adapted the game like this:

1 Centre player(first child) drops the bean bag behind another child in the circle, and runs round circle.
2 The second child picks up the bean bag and runs round the circle after the first child.
3 The first child takes the second child's place in the circle.
4 The second child drops the bean bag behind another child and so on until all have had a turn.

Circular chair

Age range	4+

Method

1 The children stand in a tight circle, all facing the same way, ie, towards the back of the person next to them.
2 They keep making the circle tighter till they are touching, then place their hands on the waist of the child in front of them and sit gently on the lap of the child behind.
Note If players are co-operating the circle will stay up and everyone will have a comfortable lap to sit on. If they do not sit down gently, the circle will fall.

Farmyard animals

Resources	Small picture cards with pictures of farm animals on. For 15 children you will need 5 pictures of 3 different animals, eg 5 sheep, 5 cows and 5 ducks
Age range	4+

Method

1 Give out the animal cards randomly, one to each child.
2 Ask children to walk around the room making the noise of their animal and listening for anyone making the same noise.
3 When they hear someone making the same noise they hold hands with them, and continue until they have found all the others making the same noise as they are.
This game can be used to sort children into groups without the need for choosing or waiting.
You will need to check first that all the children know what noise the animals pictured make.

Activities to facilitate discussion

Circle Time

In most settings children and adults come together in a group at certain points in the day. This may be for registration, 'news time', stories or songs. Circle Time can also be used as part of the process of promoting children's participation in the way the group runs and decisions that affect them.

Organising Circle Time

- For young children, 10–15 minutes is probably a realistic amount of time to set aside for each session. More than this and they may begin to get restless.
- Because young children find it hard to wait for a long while for their turn to speak, you may find it helpful to divide them into several smaller groups of 8–10 children.
- It can be useful to have some sign or symbol that indicates when Circle Time is about to take place, eg
  lighting a candle
  playing a particular piece of music
  arranging chairs or mats in a circle.
- All participants need to be at the same level – children and adults. If you sit on the floor, small carpet-sample mats, one for each child, may help the children to remain in a circle, rather than crowding forward into the centre.

Ground rules

Ground rules need to be established and explained to encourage every child to take part:

- **One person speaks at a time**
  Having a prop – such as a toy microphone, bean bag or conch shell – which the speaker must always hold, helps to reinforce this rule.

- **No interruptions**
  Everyone has a chance to complete what they wanted to say and pass on the 'prop'.

- **No one will be ridiculed or 'put down'**
  You may need to discuss with the children what 'put downs' are, how they make people feel and why they must be avoided.

- **Everyone has the right to 'pass'.**
  This means the children have the right to contribute or not, as they choose. No one will feel put on the spot.

Some ways to use Circle Time

Age range: 3+

- **For sharing feelings, ideas, experiences**
  Sometimes these will arise spontaneously from the children, or the adult may introduce a subject to the children, eg
  'One good thing that happened today'
  'A time when I felt scared'.
  Go round the circle giving each child and adult the opportunity to speak on the subject, or to pass.

- **For planning activities**
  Either short-term – what the children will do today
  or long-term – projects, outings, festivals, celebrations.

- **For discussing how the group runs**
  There might be problems with use of equipment – some children monopolising certain items; things being damaged, or lost; there might be lack of space or time for certain activities; noise levels might be too high.
  Once a problem has been identified and everyone's point of view has been heard, you could use the brainstorming technique to generate possible solutions.

- **For discussing problems concerning conflict, discipline or rules**
  Circle Time can be used to discuss actual conflicts that have arisen: what led up to them, what happened, how people felt and how they might be resolved.
  It can be used to explore hypothetical situations suggested by adults or children – 'What might happen if …', eg Liam and Jim have made a house inside the climbing frame. Hannah and Amy want to come in. Liam and Jim say 'no'.
  Ask the children to imagine first what might happen if the argument continues. Then ask them to start again and find solutions that are peaceful and that all parties feel happy with.
  It may help to use puppets to act out possible scenarios.
  Circle Time can also be used for a general discussion of the rules you have in your group – what they are for, which ones might be negotiable and which not, how they can be enforced.

- **For developing self-esteem**
  Children can be encouraged to say things that they like about each other and about themselves.

If the adults always play a full part in contributions to Circle Time, they can make appreciative comments about any child who has not had anything positive said about him or her, without drawing attention to the fact.

Brainstorming

Brainstorming is a way of involving all members of the group who are capable of expressing themselves through language in contributing ideas.

It can be used to generate ideas, collect information and solve problems.

Age range: 5+

Ground rules for brainstorming

■ All ideas are welcomed initially without comment or discussion. The leader is an equal member of the group ie is there to facilitate the gathering of ideas and subsequent discussion – not to decide what is and is not acceptable or workable.

■ When the group evaluates the ideas, no contributor is to be 'put down'.

Organising brainstorming

■ To get the children used to the way brainstorming works, start with simple, fairly concrete examples: eg bring in an object such as a flower pot.

■ Ask the group to think of as many things they could do with that object as possible.

■ On a large sheet of paper and with a thick pen, write or draw every idea.

■ When the group is used to working in this way, you can go on to introduce a real practical problem and ask the children to brainstorm solutions.

The next stage is to evaluate the solutions offered.

■ Take each one and discuss what is good about it and what the problems, if any, might be.

■ Allow the children to explore each idea fully before you say what you think.

■ Cross off the list any ideas that everyone agrees won't work.

If everyone agrees on one of the remaining ideas the group will have achieved that rare state of agreement – consensus.

■ If not, the group will need to vote on which solution it will try first. It could do this with a show-of-hands vote, but some young children may find it hard to restrict themselves to voting for just one option.

■ If this matters to the group as a whole you could give each child a sticky label with their name on which they can stick by the solution they favour. If they change their mind as they are reminded of other options, the name will make it easier to know which label to move.

■ Keep a note of the other ideas which were considered possible in case the first solution doesn't work and you need to try alternatives.

Expressing feelings and opinions

Children can sometimes be overwhelmed by how they feel, without necessarily being able to express or name what that feeling is. This may be because of a lack of vocabulary for such feelings, or it may be because they are discouraged from expressing certain feelings – told not to shout or throw things when angry; or that 'big boys don't cry', even when they feel sad. Some children, denied the expression of feelings, may believe that they shouldn't even feel the feeling, so they try to deny it even to themselves. Others may believe they are the only ones who feel in a particular way and that there must be something wrong with them. Some children (and adults) give mixed messages about their feelings: they may laugh when they really feel scared; or feign indifference when they feel hurt.

All about me books	
Resources	scrapbook (or use Sheila Wolfendale's *All about me* books)[29]
Age range	3+
Method	Through talking, drawing pictures, choosing pictures from magazines and catalogues, choosing from photos, using happy/sad stickers, dictating their thoughts for adults to write down, children can express and record what is important to them, their likes and dislikes. • Best friends • Good things about nursery/playgroup • Bad things about nursery/playgroup • Favourite toys, games, games, foods, drinks, stories • Things that make me feel happy or 'I feel happy when ...' (or sad, scared, angry, excited, bored, lonely) • 'I like it when grown-ups ...' • 'I don't like it when grown-ups ...' Views expressed by children in their books can inform adults when they: • plan activities and menus • choose new equipment • allocate children into groups or to a 'key worker' • consider changes that may be needed in how the group runs, the role of adults within the group or their approach to children.

Telling and acting out children's own stories

Age range	3+

Method

1 Introduce the idea to the children. Ask if they would like to tell you stories which you will write down in a 'story book'. Each child could have a book of their own – or there could be a group book. If lots of children want to tell stories simultaneously, you could introduce the idea of a story list, on which you or they write their names when they want to tell a story.

2 When you have a number of stories ask if the children would like to act them out. Discuss with the children where and when they might do this.

3 In the place and at the time you have agreed with the children gather them all into a circle.

4 Read the first story and then either ask the storyteller which children she would like to act in her story and which parts they will play; or let the storyteller choose her role and then go round the circle giving roles to the other children. In this way, each child will have a turn in someone's story.

5 The children act out the first story and then you can repeat the process with the remaining stories. The children can expand or adapt their stories, provided they can explain to the others the changes they want to make.

6 Sometimes roles or action may become muddled and you will need to help clarify them. Children may want to tell stories like those their friends have told. You can comment on similarities but need not discourage this as 'copying'; their imitation may be a sign of friendship, or of learning a new art from others, or one idea may have sparked off another – all these are positive.

7 Try to make time each day to act out all the stories written that day.

Working as a nursery teacher with three and four year olds, Vivian had made storytelling a regular part of her classroom. She had also encouraged children to dictate their own stories to her. But, with few exceptions, the opportunities to create stories were only occasionally taken up by the children, and then usually by the girls.

One day, when Wally had spent two periods on a 'time out' chair because he could not keep himself out of trouble, Vivian, hoping to distract him from himself, asked if he would like to write a story.

Wally was surprised. 'You didn't teach me how to write yet.'

'You just tell me the story, Wally. I'll write the words,' Vivian replied.

Wally told a story about a troublemaking dinosaur who destroyed a city and was put in jail.

'Is that the end?' Vivian asked.

'He promised to be good so they let him go home and his mother was waiting', Wally added.

Vivian then asked Wally if he would like to act out the story and include other children in the performance. She reports:

It made Wally very happy, and a flurry of story writing began that continued and grew all year. The boys dictated as many stories as the girls, and we acted out each story the day it was written if we could.

Before, we had never acted out these stories. We had dramatised every other kind of printed word – fairy tales, story books, poems, songs – but it had always seemed enough just to write the children's words. Obviously it was not; the words did not sufficiently represent the action, which needed to be shared. For this alone, the children would give up play time, as it was a true extension of play. [30]

Feelings – drama

Age range 4+

Method Give the children various scenarios and feelings associated with them. eg
- Your best friend won't play with you today and you feel lonely.
- Someone has smashed the house you built and you feel angry.
- It's your birthday tomorrow and you feel really excited.
- Your mum told you she loved you this morning and you feel happy.

- Ask all the children to pretend that one of these things has happened to them and to show, through movement, facial expression and so on how they feel about it.
- Give one child a scenario, as above, and ask her to act out, without words, how she feels.
- Ask the other children to guess, first, what feelings she is expressing and then, to suggest things that might have made her feel that way.

When you ... I felt

Age range 4+

Method
- Encourage the children to talk about how it feels to be with someone who is showing strong feelings.
- 'When you .... I felt ....'
- You might refer to an incident already mentioned by the children, or you might find it useful to read a story first that features strong feelings, eg *Peter's Chair* – jealousy; *Where the Wild Things are* – anger.
- Ask for suggestions about how they deal with someone who is showing such strong feelings.

Feelings – photographs

Resources photographs of people showing different emotions, eg, happiness, sadness, anger, fear

Group size 5 children

Age range 4+

Method
1 Ask children to show each other and you how they look when they feel happy, sad, angry, scared.
2 Ask them to describe what different parts of the face or body do when they feel these things.
3 Show the children the photos, one at a time, and ask:
   - What do you think is happening in this picture?
   - How do you think this person feels?
   - What might have made her or him feel this way?
4 With the angry, sad and frightened pictures, you could ask:
   - What do you think we could do to make them feel better?
5 If the children feel there is nothing they can do, you could ask:
   - Can you think of anyone else who could help them?

Musical feelings – exploring how children feel about given situations

Resources	large paper pens blu-tack/drawing pins chalk or ropes music
Preparation	10 minutes
Age range	6+
Preparation	1 Divide the room into four sections with chalk or ropes laid on floor and give each section an 'emotion', eg happy, sad, excited, scared. 2 Draw a face representing each emotion. 3 Fix each picture in the appropriate section of the room. 4 Explain each picture to the children and get them to show how they would look if they were feeling that emotion.
Method	1 Play music and ask all children to move around the room while the music plays. 2 Stop the music, and when it stops the children stand still, and pretend to feel the emotion of the section of the room that they are in. 3 Give a situation or scenario, such as one of those suggested below, and ask each child to imagine why they might feel happy (sad etc) in that situation. The situations you give will depend on what you and the children want to explore. Examples might be: – at nursery/playgroup/school – at bedtime – in a strange place. You can use the issues raised – eg scared of being bullied in the playground – and relate them to children's rights, eg the right to feel safe. You might discuss what rights children should have, what to do and who to talk to if their rights are denied; how to support others in fighting for their rights.

This exercise was used with children aged 7-9 at an event aimed at establishing the concept of children's rights. [31]

Happy lines/sad lines

Resources	free space chalk or tape or rope 2 large face pictures, one happy, one sad
Group size	maximum 10
Age range	3+
Preparation	1 Divide space into two areas using chalk/tape/rope. 2 Give one area a happy/I like face and the other a sad/I don't like face.
Method	1 Invite children to stand on the dividing line. 2 Call out a scenario/rule/activity/piece of equipment (depending on what you want to find out about), eg What do you think about fighting? 3 Ask children to jump to the happy or sad side of the line to indicate how they feel.

Happy mats/sad mats

Resources	2 large non-slip mats 2 large face pictures, one happy, one sad
Group size	maximum 8 children
Age range	3+
Method	1 Children stand between 2 mats 2 Call out scenario (as above) 3 Children run to one of the two mats (as above).

Happy trains/sad trains

Resources	chairs arranged in two lines, like the pretend trains/buses that children create 2 large face pictures, one happy, one sad
Group size	maximum 10
Age range	2+
Method	Proceed as above with children sitting on the 'train' that expresses their feelings.

Thumbs up/thumbs down

Group size	maximum 10
Age range	2+
Method	1 Establish physical movements for happy/I like and sad/I don't like, eg – thumbs up/down – smile/frown – jump into the air/curl into a ball 2 Proceed as above, with children making the movement or gesture that expresses how they feel.

Happy masks/sad masks

Resources	2 masks per child – one happy, one sad
Group size	maximum 10
Age range	3/4+
Preparation	Children make masks by drawing, painting or sticking pictures from magazines onto circles of card or paper plates, one showing a happy face and the other a sad face.
Method	Proceed as above with children raising or putting on the mask that expresses how they feel.

Making choices

Pros and cons

Resources	large paper/flip chart felt pens
Age range	6+
Method	• This is a way of exploring several different options and considering the possible benefits and problems of each one. • To introduce this way of working it might be helpful to practise with an imaginary, though 'concrete' example: eg Let the children pretend that each is to be offered a pet. They may choose between a cat and a dog. • Ask for their immediate choice by a show of hands/by lining up behind a picture of a cat or dog/whatever method of eliciting preferences you have found works best. • Divide a large sheet of paper into four equal parts. Label as follows: (or illustrate with pictures)

cat good things	dog good things
cat bad things	dog bad things

• Ask the children to think of as many good and bad things about each animal as they can. Note these in the relevant sections on the paper. With children who cannot read, it will help if you can illustrate these points with simple pictures.
• When you have done this, ask children to show you again which they would choose. Ask if any have changed their minds, and what caused them to do so.

Toy catalogue

This method can be used to make choices about which toys to buy, where to go on an outing, etc.

Resources	pictures of equipment card sticky paper dots
Age range	3+
Preparation (30 minutes)	1 Select a range of equipment that fits within your budget. 2 Cut and mount pictures of these on individual cards.
Method	1 Tell children you want them to help choose new toys for the group. 2 Explain that you may not have enough money for all the toys they choose and that you will be buying those that most children choose and agree on after further discussion. 3 Give each child a sticky dot and ask them to stick it on the toy they would most like. 4 With older children – aged 6+ – you could go on to use the format in 'Pros and cons' to discuss the good and bad things about each chosen toy. 5 Ask the children to prioritise which toys the group should buy. This method elicits children's preferences; it does not give them an idea of the relative cost of different items and of the amount of money available to spend.

Toy shop

This method is more complicated and is suited to children who have an understanding of number and of the need to match money available to the cost of an item.

Resources	card pictures of equipment shopping baskets shop counter
Age range	5+
Preparation	1 Mount pictures of equipment on individual cards. You will need one copy of each picture for each participating child. 2 Show the cost of each card by attaching counters to each; use one counter to represent each £10. 3 Set up a shop counter with till and appoint one person as shop keeper – this could be an adult.
Method	1 Explain the purpose of the game to the children. 2 Give each child some counters, equivalent to the budget your group has to spend. 3 Explain the rules of the game – that if a child wants a toy that has – say – three counters on it she has to give the shopkeeper three of her counters. She may buy as many toys as she has counters for. 4 Give each child a shopping basket and go, as a group, to the shop. Encourage the children to look at all the options and explain any that they are not familiar with. 5 Return, as a group, to 'home base' and invite each child to show what she has chosen and to say what it would be good for and why she has chosen it. 6 Show the children's choices on a chart. This could have a column for each toy with a picture of it at the top, and a tick or stick drawing to represent each child who chose that toy. 7 Let this group of children know that everyone else in the group will be playing the same game and that when they have made their choice you will all look at the chart and see which toys most people have chosen and that these will be the toys that you will really buy for the group.

Choosing toys

A group of children aged 2,3 and 4 were given a budget of £30 – represented by 30 discs – and a toyshop catalogue and asked to choose toys for their crèche that they would all like.

The worker leading the activity describes what took place:

Michael pointed to a sand and water activity bucket and said 'I've got that at home.' The other children agreed that it would be nice to have one at the crèche for 'everyone to play with'. We counted out four 'pounds'.

Koddie pointed to a trampoline priced £39.99. The children agreed it would be nice to have at the crèche. We counted the money we had left and agreed we had not got enough.

Koddie and Matthew looked at a skittles game and said they would like to buy them. They counted out another £4 and were very pleased that they had enough money. 'Everyone can play this skittles' said Matthew.

The children came to a picture of footballs. Keylie told us, 'We haven't got enough footballs and we fight over them.' The children agreed that we could afford the ball they liked best by counting out another £4.

We came to a hoover and Keylie told the other children that, 'if we had one of them we could clean up.' The children seemed to be picking up the idea now because they were asking 'Have we got enough money to buy it?' We counted out £15 and Michael told us 'That one is lots of money.' Keylie reassured him that 'It is a big toy!'

Matthew pointed to a shopping trolley that cost £14.99. We counted out the money and found we hadn't got enough. Koddie told us 'We already have one of them.'

Matthew spotted a birthday cake and told us we could have a 'party' if we had one. We counted the money out and realised we only had £3 left and we needed one more. Koddie pointed to the community crèche money and said 'We could get one from in there.' Can't really argue with that!

We talked about how we would get to town to the shop. Koddie told us that she has been in town to buy shoes and that they had to go on the bus. The children all agreed it would be good to go on a bus.

Matthew wanted two chairs that cost £15. I explained that we had no money left. 'My mum's got £15' he told us.

The following session the four children involved in this activity went with two workers on the bus into the city centre and bought the toys and came back to share them with the other children at the crèche.

The workers comment that the activity was very rewarding, that they will do it again, and next time will give the children a bigger budget!

[Contributed by Wood End Family Project Crèche, Coventry]

Through this activity these four young children:

- chose a range of toys that were, by any yardstick, sensible good buys.
- considered the needs of the group as a whole
- communicated and negotiated with each other
- practised mathematical skills in counting out the money, matching it to the toys they were interested in, and recognising quantity – it was the two year old who commented that the hoover is 'lots of money'
- learnt something about budget constraints and the relative cost of different toys
- exercised the right to make choices about new equipment they would have in their crèche.

Exploring specific issues

Looking at conflict – using puppets

Resources	two puppets
Age range	3+
Method	If children are arguing about, for instance, 'who started it': 1 Ask the children to tell you what happened while you re-enact the scene with the puppets. 2 Hearing the puppets repeat their words gives the children a chance to hear their opponent's point of view more dispassionately and to evaluate their own attitudes. 3 Ask the children to help the puppets find a way to settle the dispute that both puppets will feel is fair, and in which neither is the loser. 4 Use the puppets to try out each suggested solution.

This technique was piloted with two groups in Hull. In one group it worked as described; in the other the children liked the puppets fighting, wanted them to continue doing so, and were not interested in suggesting peaceful solutions.

Looking at conflict – using stories

Resources	a story in which there are two groups with conflicting interests
Age range	4+
Method	1 Tell the story, giving the children the opportunity to identify with each group in turn. 2 Stop the story at a point where the conflict of interests is evident and ask the children to think of ways in which each side might deal with it. 3 Discuss the suggestions. The children can divide into groups and act out some of the suggestions made.

Looking at rules – the 'naughty puppet'

Resources	a puppet
Age range	2+

Method	1 Introduce to the children a 'naughty puppet' who doesn't know the rules of your group and does 'naughty' things.
	2 Ask the children to tell the puppet off when it does something it shouldn't or doesn't do something it should.
	3 Listen carefully to the language children use and the explanations – if any – that they give to the puppet. You may learn not only which rules they know but also:
	  – what your own requests and explanations sound like to them
	  – how they interpret what you say
	  – ways in which you could phrase requests and explanations so that the children would find them acceptable/understandable.

Looking at rules – the fishing game

Resources	card
	paper clips
	magnet
	string
	6' length dowel
	2 boxes or nets
Age range	3+
Preparation (40 minutes)	1 Cut fish shapes out of card.
	2 Write one rule on each card. Include some rules that you do not have in your group.
	3 Attach a paper clip to each fish and make a 'fishing rod' by attaching a magnet to the dowel with a length of string.
Method	1 One child catches a 'fish'.
	2 The rule is read out by an adult and the children are asked if this is a rule that belongs to this group.
	3 If it is, it is put in one box (or net, to continue the fishing theme). If not, it is put in another box/net.
	4 The next child catches a fish, and so on.

Discussing the rules

Playing the game outlined above will simply give information as to which rules the children are aware of. You could go on to encourage discussion of the rules:

– why your group has the rules it does
– does everyone stick to the rules?
– are there any rules you group would like to 'give away'?
– are there any rules they would like to add?

Looking at rules – a card game

Resources	blank playing cards or similar size cards (see 'Resources' for suppliers)
	either 2 magnetic boards and tape *or* 2 boxes or baskets
	a list of your group rules
Group size	maximum 6
Age range	4+
Preparation	approximately 30 minutes
	(more if you have to compile a list of your rules)
	1 Write your group rules on the cards – one rule per card.
	2 Think of some rules you do not have in your group and write these on other cards.
	3 If using magnetic boards, attach magnetic tape to the back of each card.
	4 Label one board as belonging to your group, and the other not. You could use the name of your group or a photo.
Method	1 Place the playing cards in a pile on a table.
	2 One child takes the top card and an adult – or a child – reads the rule on it aloud.
	3 The children are asked if this rule belongs to their nursery/group.
	4 If it does, it is placed on one board, if not, on the other.
	5 The next child takes a card and so on.

The game can be extended by incorporating a dice and marking each card with a number of dots, arranged as they are on a dice. The cards are sorted into six piles according to the number of dots on each.

A child throws the dice, chooses a card with the same number of dots, and the game proceeds as before.

The same information is conveyed, but the use of a dice gives children the chance to sort, match and count, and makes it more like a recognisable game.

Who we like to be with – 1

Resources	photos of each child and adult in your group visual scenarios of group activities, eg – meal times: a picture of table and chairs – home corner: a photo of it without children in
Group size	1 child at a time
Age range	2+
Method	Invite child to place her own photo on one chair/at the activity and to choose from other photos whom she would like to be with her.

Who we like to be with – 2

Resources	photos (as above) with paper clip on each visual scenarios (as above) 'fishing rod', a stick attached to a magnet with string
Group size	5 children
Age range	3+
Method	Give each child in turn a scenario and ask them to 'catch' the photos of the people they would like to be with in the given scenario. *Note* You may have concerns about the feelings of a child who is never chosen. While this may be a valid reason for not using this technique, it could be argued that these children are aware that this is happening anyway in 'real life'. This technique could give an opportunity to: • discuss with all the children involved how it feels never to be chosen – or be chosen last • look at why a child is not chosen and, if necessary, plan strategies to develop any skills she is lacking, such as the ability to share or communicate; or to help her control behaviour that other children may find off-putting • explore what that child is good at and include activities/scenarios that would make use of these skills.

Who we like to be with

The Partnership in Childcare Project in Dunfermline, Fife, adapted this technique for children in their group aged 18 months to 3 years.

Having informed parents of their plans, they used photos of each child and member of staff and made them into stick puppets which were available to the children throughout the day. The staff introduced the puppets to the children and then observed them playing with the puppets over a period of eight days.

The children used the puppets in various ways:

- an 18 month old child tried to comfort a 2½ year old by giving the upset child the stick puppet of the upset child
- some children talked to and kissed the stick puppet depicting one member of staff
- one child used the puppets as dolls and placed random puppets in the pram and took them for a walk.

Adult roles

Resources	a photograph of each adult in your group a tape recorder an 'interviewer' – an adult or older child who is not part of your group
Group size	5 children
Age range	4+
Method	1 The 'interviewer' explains that she wants to find out what the grown-up people do and she hopes the children will help her. She will show them some photos, and when they see the photo they mustn't say who it is – they must just think who it is. If they don't know, that's OK, that will still help her. 2 The interviewer shows one photo and when all children have seen it, she asks each in turn to whisper in her ear the name of the person in the photo. (The whispering ensures that children don't just repeat what they have heard others say.) 3 This process is repeated with the other photos. 4 The interviewer then tells the children she is going to ask them another question, and this time she will record their answers so she doesn't forget what they say. 5 She shows each photo again and asks what the children think this person does in the group. Their answers are recorded. When this method was used with groups of 5-7 year olds just three photos were used at a time – some children were becoming restless by the end of the third photo. Children's comments included such things as: 'shouts at you', 'is kind', 'talks to you if you're feeling sad'. [32]

Designing a play area

Resources	*either* an empty sand/water tray *or* a large shallow cardboard box *or* planks of wood to define a scale version area on site
	a selection of the following: earth, sand, stones, moss, twigs, flowers, plasticine and/or clay, pipe cleaners, soft wire, straw, string, tape, netting from fruit containers, small boxes and tubes, bottle tops, toy car tyres
	camera

Group size	maximum 5 at a time

Age range	3+

Preparation	a plan of the area with any fixed existing features
	gathering materials to use in model
	taking children to other play areas to gain ideas

Method

1 Tell children that a play area is to be made in their group/neighbourhood.

2 They will not be able to build the play area itself, but they can make a model using the sand tray (box etc) and materials to show how they would like it to look and what they would like in it.

3 Demonstrate how plasticine can be used to stick 'trees' in or to anchor or join climbing structures; how netting could be hung for climbing on; car tyres arranged for climbing or planting things in; boxes used to represent play houses etc.

4 Let them know they can try things out, change them around, keep working on it until it is how they want it.

5 Explain that it will be best if they work together and talk about their ideas, because the play area will have to be something they all agree on.

6 Observe as the children work on their model and note comments they make about what their structures represent and reasons for the choices they are making.

7 Give advice or help as necessary to enable them to reach their aim.

8 Take photos – or get the children to do so – as the model progresses. It is likely to change over time and as different groups of children work on it, and a record of various plans may be helpful.

9 Involve the children in ongoing discussions about their model and let them know if any of their ideas are impractical because of space, cost or safety considerations.

10 Once the final plan has been agreed with everyone, let the children know that the play area will be built to look as much like their model as possible – that they have designed their own play area.

11 If any alterations have to be made, tell the children what these are and why.

12 Arrange site visits while the play area is being constructed so that the children can see their ideas taking shape.

Evaluating the group

Questionnaire

Resources	Children who do not yet read and write will need help with this – someone to read the opening phrases and write down their responses. As the children will be commenting on the adults in their group as well as the group itself, this will need to be someone other than their nursery or playgroup worker or teacher. It could be an older child, a student on placement or the child's parent(s).
Age range	4–7
Method	Where there are a number of adults occupying the same role in a group it will be easier if they are identified by name rather than by their role. 'I like my teacher when ...' 'The worst part of the day at nursery is ...' 'I think we should be allowed to ...' 'I wish my teacher would ...' 'The best thing about nursery is ...' 'School would be better if ...' and other questions you wish to ask.

Taped interviews

Resources	Tape recorder The interviews will need to be conducted by a 'third party', as above.
Age range	3+
Method	Adapt the phrases into questions. eg, 'When do you like your teacher best?' 'What is the worst part of the day at nursery?' 'Is there anything you want to do at nursery that you are not allowed to?' 'What do you come to nursery for?' 'Is there anything you would like your teacher to do ... or not to do?' 'What is the best thing about nursery?' 'Can you think of anything that would make nursery better?'

Good things/bad things

Resources	flip chart and pens
	card
	sticky paper dots
Group size	maximum 15
Age range	6+
Method	Brainstorm

Brainstorm
- Ask children to call out:
  what is good about this school/group
  what is bad
- Write down every suggestion on large paper. At this point, discourage any discussion.
- Merge similar bad points and write each point onto separate cards. (If you can find a way of illustrating the points visually this will help the younger, pre-literate children to participate directly.)

Prioritise
- Give each child a certain number of sticky paper dots and ask them to place dots on what the worst things are/what they would most like to change.

Taking action
- Take the number 1 priority, ie the card with the most dots.
- Ask the children to suggest things that could be done to address this issue – 'What could we do about this?'
- Review and evaluate the list of suggestions with the group of children – some suggestions may have to be discarded as unrealistic.
- Ask if they can think of any difficulties in carrying out each suggestion on the list, eg would cost too much money, could be dangerous, there isn't enough space, people would have to agree to work together.
- Can these be overcome?
- Decide to work on one suggestion – the one that seems most practical.

Picture game – to find out what children think about the activities

Resources	camera and film
	activities to photograph
	card and split pin (to secure pointer)
Age range	2–4
Method	

Method
1. Explain to children that you would like them to help make a game to tell you what they like and don't like about their crèche/nursery/playgroup.
2. Ask the children to take photos of each of the activities available. You will need to encourage them to take one photo of each – rather than several of, for instance, their favourite activity – in order to show all the activities available.
3. Develop photos and arrange on a board with a description underneath of what the activity is. Put a pointer – like a clock hand – in the middle.
4. Ask the children questions and use the pointer to illustrate their answers, eg
'What do you like about the group?'
'What don't you like about the group?'
'What is the best thing about the group?'
By involving the children in the planning and preparation for this activity, more interest, general communication and specific feedback was generated than if an adult had presented a ready-made game to the children.

This game was devised, piloted and contributed by Langley Children's Project, Middleton.

Beans in jars – quantitative evaluation

Resources	jars dried beans (for safety – not red or black kidney beans) written or photo/picture labels
Age range	5+
Preparation	1 Set out as many jars as there are things you want to evaluate 2 Label each with one aspect of your provision such as the routines of the day (indoor play, outdoor play, story time, lunchtime, going home time)
Method	Give each child a handful of beans and ask them to put 1-5 beans in each jar to show how highly they rate that aspect of their group *Note* This method, which gives a numerical score, is useful as a way of assessing how things have changed since you last evaluated using the same method.

Me at nursery (playgroup/childminder)

Resources	paper and paints/felt tip pens one-to-one attention from an adult
Age range	2+
Method	1 Ask children to do a drawing or painting of 'me at nursery' (or playgroup, school, childminder's). 2 Discuss these drawings/paintings with them – listening carefully to find out what is really important to them.

Appendix

Legislation concerning children's employment and education – a summary

Legislation	Main purpose	Outcome
1802 Health and Morals of Apprentices Act	Children from workhouses not to work . more than 12 hours a day	Not effective; there were no inspectors to ensure the Act was enforced.
1819 Factory Act	No children under nine to work in factories. Children aged nine to sixteen to work no more than 12 hours a day.	Not effective; no birth certificates were issued until 1836, so children's ages could not be checked.
1833 Factory Act	No child under nine to be employed in factories. Children aged nine to thirteen to work no more than 9 hours a day. Children aged thirteen to eighteen to work no more than 12 hours a day.	Government inspectors appointed to ensure the Act was enforced.
1842 Mines Act	No children to work underground.	
1844 Factory Act	Children aged nine to thirteen to work no more than 6.5 hours a day. Children aged thirteen to eighteen to work no more than 12 hours a day.	
1858 Government Commission to investigate schooling	Finds that only one child in 8 attends some kind of school; 80% of these leave before they are twelve.	
1870 Education Act	School places should be provided for all children. School Boards to be set up to organise this.	Parents had to pay for these and the fees plus loss of children's earnings meant many families could not afford for their children to go to school.
1876 Education Act	A duty is put on all parents to send their children to school. No child under ten is to be employed. No child over ten to be employed unless they have attended school.	
1880 Education Act	School attendance to be compulsory for children aged five to thirteen. Occasional exemptions to be made for children over ten.	
1891 Education Act	Board school fees abolished.	
1901 Factory and Workshops Act	No child under twelve to be employed.	
1902 Education Act	School Boards abolished and responsibility for providing education is given to county councils and boroughs- Local Education Authorities. LEAs could provide grammar schools offering education to sixteen+.	Entry to grammar schools restricted to those who could afford fees or gain scholarships.
1918 Education Act	School leaving age raised to fourteen.	
1944 Education Act	Free education for all. Fee paying to grammar schools abolished. Nursery schools could be provided. School leaving age to be raised first to fifteen (happened in 1947) then to sixteen as soon as possible (happened in 1973).	

References

1   Responsibility for under-eights: a guide to the law, *Starting Points 23*, Nicola Wyld, National Early Years Network, 1996

2   Article 31 Action Pack, Children's Rights and Children's Play, Play-Train, 1995

3   Children's Participation: from tokenism to citizenship, Roger Hart, Innocenti Essays, UNICEF, 1992

4   Eight rungs on the ladder of citizen participation, S R Arnstein, *Journal of the American Institute of Planners*, 1979

5   'The Use of PCA for paediatric post-operative pain management' Noelle Llewellyn, *Paediatric Nursing 5*, 1993

6   'Carrying messages home' Carey Newson. *Co-ordinate 46*, National Early Years Network. Child-to-Child Trust, Institute of Education, Bedford Way, London WC1H 0AL phone: 0171 612 6647

7   'Who cares for the young carers?' Lyn Strongin Dodds. *Co-ordinate 45*, National Early Years Network

8   'Child Workers in Asia Newsletter' Bangkok.

9   *Centuries of childhood*, Philippe Ariés

10 *Dream Babies*, Christina Hardyment. O.U.P. 1983

11 *Centuries of childhood*, Philippe Ariés

12 *A century of childhood*, Humphries, Mack etc

13 *One False Move: A Study of Children's Independent Mobility*, Hillman H, Adams J, Whitelegg J, Policy Studies Institute, 1990

14 *Escape from Childhood*, John Holt

15 *Young Children Learning*, Tizard and Hughes

16 *Working with Young Children*, Jennie Laishley

17 *Working with Young Children*, Jennie Laishley

18 *You can't say you can't play*, Vivian Gussin Paley, Harvard University Press, 1992

19 *Mollie is Three*, Vivian Gussin Paley, University of Chicago Press 1986

20 Child-to-Child, *Co-ordinate* 46

21 *Co-ordinate 45*, January 1995, Carey Newson, National Early Years Network

22 *Threads of Thinking*, Cathy Nutbrown.

23 *Extending thought in young children*, Chris Athey

24 High/Scope Institute UK, 190-192 Maple Road London SE20 8ET; phone 0181 676 0220

25 *Co-ordinate 45*, January 1995 Carey Newson, National Early Years Network

26 *Mollie is Three*, Vivian Gussin Paley, University of Chicago Press 1986

27 *Dibs in search of self*, Virginia Axline

28 Giving the young child a voice, *Co-ordinate* 45

29 Sheila Wolfendale's *All about me* books

30 *Wally's Stories* and *Mollie is Three*, Vivian Gussin Paley

31 *Empowering children and young people: a training manual for promoting involvement in decision-making*, Phil Treseder, published by Save the Children and the Children's Rights Office.

32 *Children UK*, Mhemooda Malek, Autumn 1995 National Children's Bureau.